Reconstruction in Retrospect

Reconstruction in Retrospect

Views from the Turn of the Century

Edited by
RICHARD N. CURRENT

LOUISIANA STATE UNIVERSITY PRESS
Baton Rouge
1969

Introduction

RICHARD N. CURRENT

The turn of the century was a turning point in the history of black Americans. As of 1900 they were approaching the nadir of their existence as freemen, the lowest level since the slavery period, and they were soon to begin a long, slow, halting climb toward something like equality with whites.

The prospects for ascending, even so gradually, were not yet apparent as the twentieth century opened, but the signs of recent and continuing decline were plain to see. No more than a memory any longer, after the lapse of twenty-five or thirty years, were the days of Reconstruction, when Negroes had voted and held office in the Southern states and had even represented those states in the national Congress (only two Negroes in the Senate, more than a dozen in the House of Representatives). True, the great charters of human rights still stood as documents of the Reconstruction era—the Thirteenth, Fourteenth, and Fifteenth amendments to the federal Constitution, which ostensibly provided freedom, citizenship, and the franchise for the former slaves. The Supreme Court, however, had virtually annulled

v

these guarantees by its decisions of the 1880's and 1890's. Meanwhile, employers of Negroes had reduced them to peonage if not to slavery in many parts of the South. Local custom and state law had made segregation almost complete, consigning the Negroes to schools, railroad cars, and other public facilities separate from and inferior to those enjoyed by the white community. Intimidation and trickery had kept more and more blacks away from the polls, and now, as the old century ended, state laws and constitutional amendments were finishing the job of Negro disfranchisement.

By 1900 comparatively few whites inside or outside the South were in a mood to protest very strongly against what was happening to the Negroes in that section. Among Northerners the humanitarian concern for the freedmen which the Civil War had heightened—and which, along with other interests, had motivated Radical reconstruction—was at a low ebb. After the adoption of the Fifteenth Amendment in 1870, most of the reformers had convinced themselves that their campaign in behalf of the Negro was over, that with the vote he could henceforth take care of himself, that the rest of the task of betterment was his alone. Tired white idealists could at last retire from their labors with a good conscience, and when the Negro, even with the vote, failed to improve his lot very much, many of these idealists could but reflect that perhaps they all along had overestimated his capabilities.

The Spanish-American War and the ensuing imperialist frenzy had the effect of confirming doubts about the capacity of the Negro, especially about his capacity for self-government. Imperialists used racist arguments to justify the subjection of Puerto Ricans and Filipinos to colonial rule and Cubans to the restraints of a protectorate. "Take up the white man's burden," Rudyard Kipling counseled the American people from the other side of the Atlantic in 1899. "The question is elemental. It is racial," Albert J. Beveridge told them from the Senate floor. Appeals of that kind had an obvious bearing on attitudes toward dark-skinned people at home as well as abroad. If the "little brown brother" in the Philippines needed, for his own good, the firm hand of the master race, so did the black brother in the Southern states. From 1899 to 1901 American troops were fighting in the Philippines to put down an insurrection and quiet the Filipinos' aspirations for independence. Surely the politicians of the contemporary South, in disfranchising the Negro by peaceful, orderly, legal means, were engaged in an at least equally meritorious work.

In those days Negro inferiority was not only a political slogan and a popular belief; it was also an academic doctrine. At Columbia University, for example, the political scientist John W. Burgess spoke learnedly about the inherent qualities and relative merits of the races—"Teutonic," "Celtic," "Latin," "Greek," "Slavic," and (the lowest, of course) "negro"—and warned against the granting of political rights to "barbaric populations." At Yale the social scientist William Graham Sumner emphasized cultural rather than biological inheritance, and he had little to say about contemporary American race relations in the epoch-making study he undertook in 1899 and published as *Folkways* in 1906, yet he made his feelings on the subject adequately clear in a few terse sentences: "The humanitarians of the nineteenth century did not settle anything. The contact of two races cannot be settled by any dogma. Evidence is presented every day that the problems are not settled and cannot be settled by dogmatic and sentimental generalities."

Even Negro leaders themselves were inclined to accept, at least for the time being, a rather humble position for their people. The outstanding spokesman for the blacks Booker T. Washington, in his famous Atlanta address of 1895, said nothing to discourage the accelerating trend toward segregation and disfranchisement by law. Instead, he advocated the temporary sacrifice of social privilege in exchange for economic opportunities.

He urged upon his followers "the importance of cultivating friendly relations with the Southern white man" and "interlacing our industrial, commercial, civil, and religious life" with his. "In all things that are purely social we can be as separate as the fingers, yet one as the hand in all things essential to mutual progress."

Historians reflected and reaffirmed the end-of-the-century mood as they looked back upon the events of the previous generation. Scholars such as James Ford Rhodes and William A. Dunning, in writing about Reconstruction, were telling a story with an obvious moral, namely, that the effort to make citizens and voters out of newly emancipated slaves had been a ghastly mistake. The main outlines of the story, according to the Rhodes and Dunning pattern, were as follows:

 President Lincoln had offered a generous peace, "with malice toward none, with charity for all," and his successor Andrew Johnson attempted to carry out Lincoln's plan. Before the end of 1865 the Southern states had accepted defeat and chosen reunion by disavowing their ordinances of secession, repudiating their war debts, and ratifying the Thirteenth Amendment, which would abolish slavery. However, the President's work was frustrated by the Radical Republicans in Congress. Motivated by fanaticism, vindictiveness, and partisan interest, these Radicals denied admittance to the duly elected senators and representatives from the South. The Radicals then got busy with a scheme of their own, which they imposed upon the defeated states in 1867. Under the Radical plan those states were subjected temporarily to military rule and compelled to disfranchise the former masters and enfranchise the former slaves. The reorganized governments were turned over to the Negroes and to those white men who could and would cooperate with them—newly arrived political adventurers from the North (the carpetbaggers) and degraded persons already residents of the South (the scalawags). The ignorant Negroes and their self-seeking,

unscrupulous abettors proceeded to plunder the states in an un-
believable orgy of corruption, ruinous taxation, and astronomi-
cal increases in the public debt. Respectable white men had to resort to such extra-legal organizations as the Ku Klux Klan for the
protection of their property, their lives, and above all the virtue
of their womenfolk. This horrible time was finally brought to an
end through the determination and dedication of most white
Southerners, together with the gradual disillusionment of a majority of Northerners. In 1877, with the removal of the last of
the federal troops, "white supremacy" and "home rule" and
sound government were restored throughout the South.

That view of Reconstruction history was to persist for decades. It was carried to extremes by popular writers such as the
preacher-turned-novelist Thomas Dixon and the Democratic
party propagandist Claude G. Bowers. Dixon's best-selling novel
The Clansman (1909) and the even more influential movie ver-
sion of it, *The Birth of a Nation* (1916), were melodramas of
Southern white virtue in conflict with Negro and carpetbag
vice. Bowers' *The Tragic Era* (1928), the most widely read of all
presumably nonfictional accounts of Reconstruction, depicted
the same sort of heroes and villains in equally stark confronta-
tion. Professional historians usually wrote with more qualification and restraint but continued to present an essentially similar
story. In the 1920's and 1930's two of them, Charles A. Beard and
Howard K. Beale, added to the Dunning interpretation by elab-
orating upon Northern business interests as presumed motivating
forces back of Radical Reconstruction.

Among historians, however, there was already a growing
number of dissenters. A pioneer of the revisionist movement was
the Negro scholar W. E. Burghardt Du Bois. In 1909 (the year
that Dixon's *The Clansman* appeared) Du Bois presented, at the
annual meeting of the American Historical Association, a paper
in which he pointed out that the evils of Reconstruction had
been exaggerated and its positive achievements overlooked. In

1940 Beale called for a reconsideration of the period and indicated some of the lines of inquiry that historians might profitably pursue. During the next generation a great many took up the challenge, among them John Hope Franklin, C. Vann Woodward, Kenneth M. Stampp, David Donald, Eric McKitrick, W. L. Brock, and John and La Wanda Cox. These writers did not agree among themselves on every point, but they were unanimous in believing that the traditional view of Reconstruction was defective in many if not most respects.

The more recent historians came to new conclusions not only because of additional research but also because of a changed perspective. During the first half of the century, the *Zeitgeist*—which historians reflect—obviously underwent a profound transformation. Though racism persisted as a popular belief, it ceased to have the sanction of academic authority. A comparison of white and Negro scores on tests given to American recruits of the First World War indicated that intellectual ability was a function of individual capacity and cultural opportunity, not of racial inheritance. During the postwar years, anthropologists, sociologists, and psychologists confirmed that conclusion. Later the Nazis, by carrying their kind of racism to its logical end, made all such doctrines at least a little embarrassing. After the Second World War, with the breakup of empires and the conversion of colonies into nations, it was no longer possible, as it had been in the heyday of imperialism, to point to the dominance of light over dark peoples as an evidence of racial superiority and inferiority. As American Negroes took up the struggle for civil rights, often against brutal repression, they aroused the sympathy of many in the white community, including historical scholars. The Negroes, by their action, also demonstrated the falsity of the old stereotype that had characterized them as inherently passive, contented, and carefree.

These changes in attitude toward race are reflected in the new, revisionist history of Reconstruction. The recent historians assume that the freedmen of the 1860's and 1870's, despite the handicaps of their previous servitude, were by nature quite capable of participating in self-government. The revisionists differ most fundamentally from their predecessors in a relative lack of race bias.

According to the revisionists, most of the earlier writers were guilty of exaggeration and distortion in regard to almost every major phase of the Reconstruction story. President Johnson, by obstructing relatively mild measures, was himself to blame for bringing on much of the harshness of the ultimate congressional plan. But that plan was not really very harsh—seldom if ever in all history did the losers in a civil war get off so easily as the defeated Confederates did. Actually, the vast majority of the former rebels suffered no legal penalties whatsoever. Even the leaders were proscribed only partially and temporarily, and after 1872 only a handful of them continued to be deprived of any political rights. All that most of them really lost, through the postwar politics of the federal government, was their property in slaves.

The Radical Republicans were not united by any set of economic interests. To the extent that the Radicals made up a cohesive group, they were brought together by a common determination to secure the war aims of union and freedom. To be assured of freedom, the Negroes had to be guaranteed at least a few minimal rights. This, the question of civil rights for Negroes, was the basic issue between Johnson and the Democrats on the one hand and all but a few of the Republicans on the other. If Johnson had had his own way, the former slaves would have been remanded to a new servitude scarcely different from the old. Such was the condition provided for them in the black codes which the Southern states adopted and Johnson tolerated in 1865–1866. Much of the work of the Freedmen's Bureau consisted in counteracting those codes.

In the reconstructed states, there was little if anything that could properly be called "Negro rule." In only two of the states was there ever a Negro majority in either branch of the legislature, and in none of them was a Negro ever elected governor. Neither did the Negroes monopolize the government jobs—they received much less than a proportionate share of them—nor did they obtain more than a few unimportant state laws discriminating in their favor. As for the carpetbaggers, many if not a majority of them were comparatively high-minded and well-educated men who went south (before 1867) as settlers and took a good deal of capital with them. And as for the scalawags, they included some of the wealthiest and most respectable of the planters and businessmen, as well as ordinary persons who had never been slaveowners. The Negro-carpetbag-scalawag governments did indeed increase expenditures, taxes, and debts, but not so fantastically as has been alleged, nor was all the money misspent: much of it went into the improvement of transportation and the provision of public schools, which had been lacking in most of the South before the war.

Some of the revisionist writing led to the conclusion that the mistake in Reconstruction was not the attempt to confer civil and political rights upon Negroes, but the failure to provide an adequate economic and educational basis and adequate governmental protection for the assurance of those rights. Yet, as one of the newer historians, Kenneth M. Stampp, pointed out, the reconstruction effort, as viewed in the larger perspective, was not an utter failure. After all, it produced the Fourteenth and Fifteenth amendments, and although these remained dead letters year after year, they were eventually revived to form the constitutional basis for the civil rights movement that began to gain momentum at the middle of the twentieth century.

In 1901, at that earlier turning point in Negro history, one of the nation's oldest and most respected magazines, the *Atlantic Monthly*, ran a series of articles on Reconstruction. The authors represented a fairly wide range of backgrounds and, for that time, a considerable diversity of outlooks. Five were Southerners by birth and upbringing, and five (counting the editor of the magazine, who provided a concluding commentary) were Northerners. The latter included the influential historian of reconstruction William A. Dunning, the rising Negro scholar W. E. Burghardt Du Bois, and one of the most prominent of former carpetbaggers, Daniel H. Chamberlain.

One of the Southerners was Woodrow Wilson, a 45-year old professor at Princeton (and soon to be president of the University). Born in Virginia, Wilson had grown up in Georgia and the Carolinas during the period of war and reconstruction. After attending Davidson College for a time, he transferred to Princeton and there obtained his bachelor's degree. He studied law at the University of Virginia, practiced briefly as a lawyer in Georgia, and then enrolled as a graduate student in political science at the Johns Hopkins University, which awarded him the Ph.D. in 1886. He taught at Bryn Mawr College and Wesleyan University before joining the Princeton faculty in 1890. By 1901 he already had two books to his credit: *Congressional Government* (1885), a scholarly study of enduring merit; and *The State* (1888), a political science textbook. Though he had done no firsthand research in Reconstruction history, he was certainly competent for his *Atlantic Monthly* assignment, the writing of an interpretive essay on the broad constitutional aspects of Reconstruction.

When Alabama-born Hilary A. Herbert wrote his *Atlantic* essay on Southern conditions from 1865 to 1867, he was a Washington lawyer, about sixty-seven years old, with a notable record as a politician and as a propagandist for the South. Herbert had studied at the universities of Alabama and Virginia. He had seen active service in the Confederate army, rising to the rank of colonel, and had practiced law in Alabama during Reconstruction. From 1877 to 1893 he served in Congress as a Democratic representative from Alabama, and from 1893 to 1897 was Secretary of the Navy in President Grover Cleveland's cabinet, distinguishing himself as a big-navy advocate. Meanwhile, he edited and contributed a chapter to one of the most influential books ever written on Reconstruction: *Why the Solid South? or, Reconstruction and Its Results* (1890). This book, directed primarily at Northern businessmen, was intended to turn them against and thus to defeat a bill then pending in Congress for the enforcement of the Fifteenth Amendment in the South. (The bill failed to pass.)

W. E. Burghardt Du Bois was a young professor of economics and history at Atlanta University when he wrote on the Freedmen's Bureau for the *Atlantic* series. Du Bois had been born in Massachusetts in 1868, too late to have had any direct, personal acquaintance with his subject. He was, however, a historian of proven ability. He held both a bachelor's and a doctor's degree from Harvard, and his dissertation, *The Suppression of the African Slave-Trade to the United States of America, 1638–1870* (1896), was an excellent piece of work (more than seventy years after its publication it was still to be considered the best account of the foreign slave trade). He was also the author of *The Philadelphia Negro* (1899). By the age of thirty-three, he had already demonstrated many of the qualities that were to make him, in the more than sixty years remaining to him, a pathbreaking student of Negro life and one of the foremost leaders of the Negro people, one far more militant than Booker T. Washington had been.

Daniel H. Chamberlain, sixty-six and living in retirement on the Massachusetts farm where he had been born, wrote from bitter personal experience in his *Atlantic* essay on Reconstruction in South Carolina. Chamberlain had graduated from Yale and was a student at the Harvard Law School when, in 1863, he withdrew from his studies to serve as a lieutenant (later a captain) of colored troops. Visiting South Carolina after the war, in 1866, he remained to try his hand at planting cotton. As a Republican, he served as attorney general of the state from 1868 to 1872 and as governor from 1874 to 1877. He claimed reelection in 1876, but the election was contested by the Democrats, whose candidate was the former Confederate war hero Wade Hampton, and who had the backing of a private army, the Red Shirts. When the incoming Republican President Rutherford B. Hayes, in effect chose Hampton over Chamberlain and removed the small federal military guard from the statehouse, Chamberlain had no choice but to give up the gubernatorial office. Shortly afterward, Chamberlain denounced Hayes's Southern policy, saying that it amounted to "the abandonment of Southern Republicans, and especially the colored race, to the control and rule not only of the Democratic party, but of that class at the South which regarded slavery as a Divine Institution, which waged four years of destructive war for its perpetuation, which steadily opposed citizenship and suffrage for the Negro." Soon he took up the practice of law in New York City. By 1901, he had almost completely reversed his attitude toward Reconstruction.

William Garrott Brown, born and brought up in Alabama, held A.B. and A.M. degrees from Harvard and was a 33-year-old assistant in the Harvard library when his essay on the Ku Klux Klan appeared in the *Atlantic*. He had already produced one book, *Andrew Jackson* (1900), and was at work on another, *The Lower South in American History* (1902).

S. W. McCall was a Republican congressman from Massachusetts at the time he undertook to defend the Radical Reconstruction policy in the pages of the *Atlantic*. Born in Pennsylvania in 1851, McCall had been reared in Illinois and, after graduating from Dartmouth, had begun to practice law in Boston. He was elected to the Massachusetts legislature three times and then to the national Congress ten times. From 1916 to 1918 he was governor of Massachusetts. The first of his four books was a sympathetic biography of the Pennsylvania Radical Republican leader, *Thaddeus Stevens* (1898).

William A. Dunning, at forty-four, was already well launched upon his influential career of teaching and writing when he contributed his essay on the undoing of Reconstruction to the *Atlantic* series. Born in New Jersey, Dunning had spent his entire life in the North. He attended Dartmouth for a time but received all his degrees—A.B., A.M., and Ph.D.—from Columbia, and he remained at Columbia throughout his teaching career, which began in 1885. To him came a number of very able graduate students, many of them from the South, who wrote dissertations on Reconstruction in various states. Before 1901 he himself had produced one book, *Essays on the Civil War and Reconstruction* (1898).

Bliss Perry, editor of the *Atlantic* since 1899, possessed a growing reputation as an essayist and literary critic at the time the Reconstruction articles appeared. Born in Massachusetts in 1860, Perry had earned a bachelor's degree at Williams and a master's at Princeton, and had taught at both places. Later (1906–1930) he was to have a distinguished career at Harvard.

As these writers looked back upon the events of a previous generation, none of them could entirely free himself from the preconceptions of the time at which he was writing. None could quite approve the unqualified enfranchisement of the former slaves. McCall—the Republican politician and admirer of Thaddeus Stevens—confesses that during Reconstruction "a point was soon reached where it became apparent that the equality established at the ballot box could be maintained only at the price of civilization." Even the Negro spokesman Du Bois concedes that if the "alternative offered the nation" had been "between full and restricted Negro suffrage," then "every sensible man, black and white, would easily have chosen the latter"—though Du Bois hastens to add that in fact it had been "rather a choice between suffrage and slavery." Readers of the *Atlantic* series were thus left to draw the conclusion that, since the wholesale creation of black voters in the South had been at best a dubious experiment, the final elimination of those voters would be at worst a necessary evil, despite the *Atlantic* editor's last word, a rather halfhearted plea for the "old faith that the plain people, of whatever blood or creed, are capable of governing themselves."

Though these writers addressed themselves to their own generation, they have something to say to ours as well. Unintentionally, they remind us of the mental climate of their time and enable us to make at least a rough judgment of the extent to which the atmosphere has changed since then. Some of them provide personal documents of a certain historical value. Thus Wilson, already the proponent and later to be the practitioner of executive authority, lets us know his feelings about a case in which the presidential power was overwhelmed by the congressional. Chamberlain, the ex-carpetbagger, though writing in "the light of retrospect and the disillusionment of later events," provides a firsthand account of his overthrow as governor of South Carolina. Du Bois approaches his subject in a spirit anticipating the one that now prevails. Indeed, despite the limitations of their time, despite the exaggerations and distortions to which most of them were prone, all the authors present insights of continuing validity (and, incidentally, all of them write remarkably well). They foreshadow a surprising number of views that have been adopted and elaborated by present-day historians of Reconstruction.

Referring to Southern attitudes shortly after the war's end, Herbert recognizes the existence of a "feeling of vindictiveness" which he says "pervaded more or less all classes who had sympathized with the Confederacy." He also notes the differences of interest and opinion, the "lines of cleavage that would inevitably have divided the Southern people into two bitterly hostile factions, had not the sempiternal negro question now appeared." Few revisionists would take issue with these observations, though they come from an ex-Confederate and a propagandist for the conservative South. Indeed, modern critics could find little to question in Herbert's entire essay—if they were to consider the essay as a summary of white conservatives' views from 1865 to 1877 and not as an objective account of the issues and events of that period.

Herbert defends the black codes as little different and no worse than New England apprentice legislation, but McCall can "find no palliation in the poor excuse that has been made for them," and even Wilson admits that in many cases they "went the length of a veritable 'involuntary servitude.'" Wilson understands that, in extending the life and powers of the Freedmen's Bureau, Congress was trying to check the operation of the black codes, was "attempting to help the negroes to make use of their freedom,—and self-defensive use of it, at that." Du Bois, in his sensitive and well-balanced essay, makes clear the essential role of the Freedmen's Bureau by placing that agency squarely in the context of its time.

In accounting for the quarrel that developed between the President and the Congress, Wilson sees and states the central issue. Lincoln's and Johnson's plan, he says, "did not meet the wishes of the congressional leaders with regard to the protection of the negroes in their new rights as freemen." The mass of Southern whites, even those who had opposed secession and later had willingly taken the loyalty oath, "would probably accept nothing but the form of freedom for the one-time slaves." All the Republican congressmen were agreed that it was properly the task of Congress to see that freedmen were "secured in the enjoyment of the equality and even the privileges of citizens, in accordance with the federal guarantee that there should be a republican form of government in every state." McCall agrees and puts the fundamental question thus: "How should the good results of the war be made permanent?" Dunning allows for "various motives" on the part of the congressional Republicans, and accepts as at least one motive the desire to secure the "result of the war."

McCall shows that the Republicans had no preconceived plan which, from the outset, they schemed to impose upon Johnson and the South. He points out, for instance, that Thaddeus Stevens was not an early advocate of Negro suffrage. Radical Reconstruction in its final and extreme form resulted from no fanatical plot, McCall argues, but from the resistance that Johnson and his adherents in the South put up against earlier and milder measures. "One event followed another, and the people of one section, no less than those of the other, are entitled to credit or blame for what occurred." Wilson cites as an example the rejection of the Fourteenth Amendment by the Southern states when it was first presented to them: "Their action confirmed the houses in their attitude toward Reconstruction." Chamberlain also explains the extremist policy as due in part to the "folly" of the South itself and to the "fatuous course of President Johnson."

Chamberlain suggests that the outcome would have been happier if Reconstruction had been entrusted to better leaders on both sides—to men like John A. Andrew, the wartime governor of Massachusetts, and Wade Hampton, the former Confederate cavalry commander from South Carolina. Chamberlain praises Andrew for his wisdom in warning, as early as 1866, that the "natural leaders" of the South must be taken into account: "Andrew pointed out, with prophetic insight, that these men, if not accepted as friends, would renew their leadership as enemies." Chamberlain lauds Hampton as one whose "strength of leadership" lay in "high and forceful character, perfect courage, and real devotion to what he conceived to be the welfare of South Carolina." (A present-day historian, Eric L. McKitrick, in his *Andrew Johnson and Reconstruction*, published in 1960, devotes a whole chapter to the might-have-beens of a Reconstruction program led jointly by Andrew and Hampton.)

Brown, a sympathizer with the Ku Klux Klan, justifies its activities as the means by which "Southern society was righted."

Nevertheless, he makes some sound observations about the Klan. "It was too widespread, too spontaneous, too clearly a popular movement," he writes, "to be attributed to any one man or to any conspiracy of a few men." The KKK itself was "only a part—and perhaps not the most important part—of the movement which in the North was called the Ku Klux conspiracy." Brown concedes that, to outsiders (who could not appreciate its indispensability), it looked like a "secret movement, operating by terror and violence to nullify laws." Chamberlain, an outsider who knew Ku Kluxism from a close view of it, forthrightly described it as "brutal and murderous," an "organized attempt to overawe and drive from office Republican state officers, and especially negroes."

Chamberlain also was blunt in summarizing the South Carolina election of 1876, which in the end he and his fellow Republicans lost. "By a system of violence and coercion ranging through all the possible grades, from urgent persuasion to mob violence and plentiful murders, the election was won by the Democrats." Dunning, though approving the outcome in South Carolina and elsewhere, frankly avows that "intimidation" was the key to Democratic success. (He justifies intimidation in Mississippi by referring to the "extravagance and corruption of the state administration," but in fact the administration of the carpetbag governor Adelbert Ames was neither extravagant nor corrupt.) Dunning is equally candid in explaining the means by which the Negroes, after the Democrats' seizure of power, were deprived of the rights that Radical Reconstruction had undertaken to assure them. Chamberlain and even Brown call attention to the unfortunate consequences of the undoing of Reconstruction—"the method of it survives in too many habits of the Southern mind," such as the propensity to defy the law and resort to lynching.

Dunning labels James G. Blaine a poor prophet for saying in 1879 that the Southern states would not dare to disfranchise Negroes by educational or property tests. But Dunning himself hardly qualifies as a dependable seer in the prediction he makes: "In view of the questions which have been raised by our lately established relations with other races, it seems most improbable that the historian will soon, or ever, have to record a reversal of the conditions which this process [the undoing of Reconstruction] has established." He is referring, of course, to the "lately established relations" with the people of Puerto Rico, the Philippines, and Cuba. Obviously, those relations are no longer what they used to be, and a reversal of the process by which Reconstruction was undone is well under way.

Du Bois envisions the future much more accurately. Not that his recommendation has yet been put into effect—his conception of a permanent Freedmen's Bureau, with the federal government providing schools, employment agencies, legal protection, banks and savings and loan associations, and social settlements for Negroes. Some comprehensive and enduring program of that kind might have "solved in a way we have not yet solved the most perplexing and persistent of the Negro problems." Du Bois is quite aware that "such an institution was unthinkable in 1870" —as it apparently will also be in 1970. But he can hardly be gainsaid when he concludes: "The problem of the twentieth century is the problem of the color line."

Seven of the nine *Atlantic Monthly* articles, together with the concluding commentary by the magazine's editor, are reprinted in the present book. The other two essays—"New Orleans and Reconstruction" by Albert Phelps and "The Southern People and Reconstruction" by Thomas Nelson Page—have been omitted on the ground that they would add little of importance, embodying as they do an extreme Southern conservative bias, which is more responsibly and authoritatively expressed in some of the seven that have been reproduced here. These seven and the *Atlantic* editor's comment are reprinted in the same order and in exactly the same form as they originally appeared, with only the following exceptions: a typographical error has been corrected in one of the articles, and several lines of the editor's comment, lines which in no way change its meaning, have been left out.

Contents

Reconstruction
in Retrospect

The Reconstruction of the Southern States

WOODROW WILSON

It is now full thirty years, and more, since the processes of reconstruction were finished, and the southern states restored to
their place in the Union. Those thirty years have counted for
more than any other thirty in our history, so great have been
the speed and range of our development, so comprehensive and
irresistible has been the sweep of change amongst us. We have
come out of the atmosphere of the sixties. The time seems remote, historic, not of our day. We have dropped its thinking,
lost its passion, forgot its anxieties, and should be ready to speak
of it, not as partisans, but as historians.

Most troublesome questions are thus handed over, sooner or
later, to the historian. It is his vexation that they do not cease to
be troublesome because they have been finished with by statesmen, and laid aside as practically settled. To him are left all the
intellectual and moral difficulties, and the subtle, hazardous, responsible business of determining what was well done, what ill
done; where motive ran clear and just, where clouded by passion, poisoned by personal ambition, or darkened by malevo-

3

lence. More of the elements of every policy are visible to him than can have been visible to the actors on the scene itself; but he cannot always be certain which they saw, which they did not see. He is deciding old questions in a new light. He is dangerously cool in dealing with questions of passion; too much informed about questions which had, in fact, to be settled upon a momentary and first impression; scrupulous in view of things which happened afterward, as well as of things which happened before the acts upon which he is sitting in judgment. It is a wonder that historians who take their business seriously can sleep at night.

Reconstruction is still revolutionary matter. Those who delve in it find it like a banked fire, still hot and fiery within, for all it has lain under the ashes a whole generation; and a thing to take fire from. It is hard to construct an argument here which shall not be heated, a source of passion no less than of light. And then the test of the stuff must be so various. The American historian must be both constitutional lawyer and statesman in the judgments he utters; and the American constitutional lawyer must always apply, not a single, but a double standard. He must insist on the plain, explicit command and letter of the law, and yet he must not be impracticable. Institutions must live and take their growth, and the laws which clothe them must be no straitjacket, but rather living tissue, themselves containing the power of normal growth and healthful expansion. The powers of government must make shift to live and adapt themselves to circumstances: it would be the very negation of wise conservatism to throttle them with definitions too precise and rigid.

Such difficulties, however, are happily more formidable in the mass than in detail; and even the period of Reconstruction can now be judged fairly enough, with but a little tolerance, breadth, and moderation added to the just modicum of knowledge. Some things about it are very plain—among the rest, that it is a period too little studied as yet, and of capital importance in our constitutional history. Indeed, it is not too much to say that there crosses it, in full sight of every one who will look, a great rift, which breaks, and must always break, the continuity and harmony of our constitutional development. The national government which came out of Reconstruction was not the national government which went into it. The civil war had given leave to one set of revolutionary forces; reconstruction gave leave to another still more formidable. The effects of the first were temporary, the inevitable accompaniments of civil war and armed violence; the effects of the second were permanent, and struck to the very centre of our forms of government. Any narrative of the facts, however brief, carries that conclusion upon its surface.

The war had been fought to preserve the Union, to dislodge and drive out by force the doctrine of the right of secession. The southern states *could* not legally leave the Union—such had been the doctrine of the victorious states whose armies won under Grant and Sherman—and the federal government had been able to prevent their leaving, in fact. In strict theory, though their people had been in revolt, under organizations which called themselves states, and which had thrown off all allegiance to the older Union and formed a new confederation of their own, Virginia, North Carolina, South Carolina, Florida, Georgia, Mississippi, Alabama, Louisiana, Texas, Arkansas, and Tennessee, the historic states once solemnly embodied in the Union, had never gone out of it, could never go out of it and remain states. In fact, nevertheless, their representatives had withdrawn from the federal House and Senate; their several governments, without change of form or personnel, had declared themselves no longer joined with the rest of the states in purpose or allegiance, had arranged a new and separate partnership, and had for four years maintained an organized resistance to the armies of the Union which they had renounced. Now that their resistance had been overcome and their confederacy destroyed, how were they to be treated? As if they had been all the while in the Union, whether they would or no, and were now at last simply brought to their senses again, to take up their old-time rights and duties intact, resume their familiar functions within the Union as if nothing had happened? The theory of the case was tolerably clear; and the Supreme Court of the United States presently supplied lawyers, if not statesmen, with a clear enough formulation of it. The Constitution, it said (for example, in the celebrated case of Texas *vs.* White, decided in 1868), had created an indestructible Union of indestructible states. The eleven states which had attempted to secede had not been destroyed by their secession. Everything that they had done to bring about secession or maintain resistance to the Union was absolutely null and void, and without legal effect; but their laws passed for other purposes, even those passed while they were in fact maintaining their resolution of secession and defying the authority of the national government, were valid, and must be given effect to in respect of all the ordinary concerns of business, property, and personal obligation, just as if they had been passed in ordinary times and under ordinary circumstances. The states had lost no legitimate authority; their acts were invalid only in respect of what they had never had the right to do.

But it was infinitely hard to translate such principles into a practicable rule of statesmanship. It was as difficult and hazardous a matter to reinstate the states as it would have been had their legal right to secede been first admitted, and then destroyed by the revolutionary force of arms. It became, whatever the theory, in fact a process of reconstruction. Had Mr. Lincoln lived, perhaps the whole of the delicate business might have been carried through with dignity, good temper, and simplicity of method; with all necessary concessions to passion, with no pedantic insistence upon consistent and uniform rules, with sensible irregularities and compromises, and yet with a straightforward, frank, and open way of management which would have assisted to find for every influence its natural and legitimate and quieting effect. It was of the nature of Mr. Lincoln's mind to reduce complex situations to their simples, to guide men without irritating them, to go forward and be practical without being radical— to serve as a genial force which supplied heat enough to keep action warm, and yet minimized the friction and eased the whole progress of affairs.

It was characteristic of him that he had kept his own theory clear and unconfused throughout the whole struggle to bring the southern people back to their allegiance to the Union. He had never recognized any man who spoke or acted for the southern people in the matter of secession as the representative of any government whatever. It was, in his view, not the southern states which had taken up arms against the Union, but merely the people dwelling within them. State lines defined the territory within which rebellion had spread and men had organized under arms to destroy the Union; but their organization had been effected without color of law; that could not be a state, in any legal meaning of the term, which denied what was the indispensable prerequisite of its every exercise of political functions, its membership in the Union. He was not fighting states, therefore, or a confederacy of states, but only a body of people who refused to act as states, and could not, if they would, form another Union. What he wished and strove for, without passion save for the accomplishment of his purpose, without enmity against persons, and yet with burning hostility against what the southerners meant to do, was to bring the people of the southern states once more to submission and allegiance; to assist them, when subdued, to rehabilitate the states whose territory and resources, whose very organization, they had used to effect a revolution; to do whatever the circumstances and his own powers, whether as President or merely as an influential man and earnest friend of peace, might render possible to put them back, defeated, but not conquered or degraded, into the old-time hierarchy of the Union.

There were difficulties and passions in the way which possibly

even Mr. Lincoln could not have forced within any plan of good
will and simple restoration; but he had made a hopeful beginning
before he died. He had issued a proclamation of amnesty so early
as 1863, offering pardon and restoration to civil rights to all who
would abandon resistance to the authority of the Union, and take
the oath of unreserved loyalty and submission which he prescribed; and as the war drew to an end, and he saw the power of
the Union steadily prevail, now here, now there, throughout an
ever increasing area, he earnestly begged that those who had
taken the oath and returned to their allegiance would unite in
positive and concerted action, organize their states upon the old
footing, and make ready for a full restoration of the old conditions. Let those who had taken the oath, and were ready to bind
themselves in all good faith to accept the acts and proclamations
of the federal government in the matter of slavery—let all, in
short, who were willing to accept the actual results of the war,
organize themselves and set up governments made conformable
to the new order of things, and he would recognize them as the
people of the states within which they acted, ask Congress to admit their representatives, and aid them to gain in all respects full
acknowledgment and enjoyment of statehood, even though the
persons who thus acted were but a tenth part of the original
voters of their states. He would not insist upon even so many as
a tenth, if only he could get *some* body of loyal citizens to deal
and coöperate with in this all-important matter upon which he
had set his heart; that the roster of the states might be complete
again, and some healing process follow the bitter anguish of the
war.

Andrew Johnson promptly made up his mind, when sum-
moned to the presidency, to carry out Mr. Lincoln's plan, practically without modification; and he knew clearly what Mr. Lincoln's plan had been, for he himself had restored Tennessee upon
that plan, as the President's agent and representative. As military
governor of the state, he had successfully organized a new gov-

ernment out of abundant material, for Tennessee was full of men who had had no sympathy with secession; and the government which he had organized had gone into full and vigorous operation during that very spring which saw him become first Vice President, and then President. In Louisiana and Arkansas similar governments had been set up even before Mr. Lincoln's death. Congress had not recognized them, indeed; and it did not, until a year had gone by, recognize even Tennessee, though her case was the simplest of all. Within her borders the southern revolt had been, not solid and of a piece, but a thing of frayed edges and a very doubtful texture of opinion. But, though Congress doubted, the plan had at least proved practicable, and Mr. Johnson thought it also safe and direct.

Mr. Johnson himself, unhappily, was not safe. He had been put on the same ticket with Mr. Lincoln upon grounds of expediency such as have too often created Vice Presidents of the United States. Like a great many other Tennesseans, he had been staunch and unwavering in his adherence to the Union, even after his state had cast the Union off; but he was in all other respects a Democrat of the old order rather than a Republican of the new, and when he became President the rank and file of the Republicans in Congress looked upon him askance, as was natural. He himself saw to it, besides, that nobody should relish or trust him whom bad temper could alienate. He was self-willed, imperious, implacable; as headstrong and tempestuous as Jackson, without Jackson's power of attracting men, and making and holding parties. At first, knowing him a radical by nature, some of the radical leaders in Congress had been inclined to trust him; had even hailed his accession to the presidency with open satisfaction, having chafed under Lincoln's power to restrain them. "Johnson, we have faith in you!" Senator Wade had exclaimed. "By the gods, there will be no trouble now in running the government!" But Johnson was careful that there should be trouble. He was determined to lead as Lincoln had led, but without Lincoln's insight, skill, or sweetness of temper—by power and self-assertion rather than by persuasion and the slow arts of management and patient accommodation; and the houses came to an open breach with him almost at once.

Moreover, there was one very serious and radical objection to Mr. Lincoln's plan for restoring the states, which would in all likelihood have forced even him to modify it in many essential particulars, if not to abandon it altogether. He had foreseen difficulties, himself, and had told Congress that his plan was meant to serve only as a suggestion, around which opinion might have an opportunity to form, and out of which some practicable method might be drawn. He had not meant to insist upon it, but only to try it. The main difficulty was that it did not meet the wishes of the congressional leaders with regard to the protection of the negroes in their new rights as freemen. The men whom Mr. Lincoln had called upon to reorganize the state governments of the South were, indeed, those who were readiest to accept the results of the war, in respect of the abolition of slavery as well as in all other matters. No doubt they were in the beginning men who had never felt any strong belief in the right of secession—men who had even withstood the purpose of secession as long as they could, and had wished all along to see the old Union restored. They were a minority now, and it might be pretty safely assumed that they had been a minority from the outset in all this fatal business. But they were white men, bred to all the opinions which necessarily went along with the existence and practice of slavery. They would certainly not wish to give the negroes political rights. They might be counted on, on the contrary, to keep them still as much as possible under restraint and tutelage. They would probably accept nothing but the form of freedom for the one-time slaves, and their rule would be doubly unpalatable to the men in the North who had gone all these weary years through, either in person or in heart, with the northern armies upon their mission of emancipation.

The actual course of events speedily afforded means for justifying these apprehensions. Throughout 1865 Mr. Lincoln pushed the presidential process of reconstruction successfully and rapidly forward. Provisional governors of his own appointment in the South saw to it that conventions were elected by the voters who had taken the oath prescribed in the amnesty proclamation, which Mr. Johnson had reissued, with little change either of form or of substance; those conventions proceeded at once to revise the state constitutions under the supervision of the provisional governors, who in their turn acted now and again under direct telegraphic instructions from the President in Washington; the several ordinances of secession were repealed, the war debts of the states were repudiated, and the legislatures set up under the new constitutions hastened to accept and ratify the Thirteenth Amendment, abolishing slavery, as the President demanded. By December of the very year of his inauguration, every southern state except Florida and Texas had gone through the required process, and was once more, so far as the President was concerned, in its normal relations with the federal government. The federal courts resumed their sessions in the restored states, and the Supreme Court called up the southern cases from its docket. On December 18, 1865, the Secretary of State formally proclaimed the Thirteenth Amendment ratified by the vote of twenty-seven states, and thereby legally embodied in the Constitution, though eight of the twenty-seven were states which the President had thus of his own motion reconstructed. Without their votes the amendment would have lacked the constitutional three-fourths majority.

The President had required nothing of the new states with regard to the suffrage; that was a matter, as he truly said, in respect of which the several states had "rightfully exercised" their free and independent choice "from the origin of the government to the present day;" and of course they had no thought of admitting the negroes to the suffrage. Moreover, the new governments, once organized, fell more and more entirely into the hands of the very persons who had actively participated in secession. The President's proclamation of amnesty had, indeed, excepted certain classes of persons from the privilege of taking the oath which would make them voters again, under his arrangements for reconstruction: those who had taken a prominent official part in secession, or who had left the service of the United States for the service of the Confederate government. But a majority of the southerners were still at liberty to avail themselves of the privilege of accepting the new order of things; and it was to their interest to do so, in order that the new arrangements might be shaped as nearly as possible to their own liking. What was to their liking, however, proved as distasteful to Congress as had been expected. The use they made of their restored power brought absolute shipwreck upon the President's plans, and radically altered the whole process of reconstruction.

An extraordinary and very perilous state of affairs had been created in the South by the sudden and absolute emancipation of the negroes, and it was not strange that the southern legislatures should deem it necessary to take extraordinary steps to guard against the manifest and pressing dangers which it entailed. Here was a vast "laboring, landless, homeless class," once slaves, now free; unpracticed in liberty, unschooled in self-control; never sobered by the discipline of self-support, never established in any habit of prudence; excited by a freedom they did not understand, exalted by false hopes; bewildered and without leaders, and yet insolent and aggressive; sick of work, covetous of pleasure—a host of dusky children untimely put out of school. In some of the states they outnumbered the whites—notably in Mississippi and South Carolina. They were a danger to themselves as well as to those whom they had once served, and now feared and suspected; and the very legislatures which had accepted the Thirteenth Amendment hastened to pass laws which should put them under new restraints. Stringent regulations were adopted with regard to contracts for labor, and with regard to the prevention of vagrancy. Penalties were denounced against those who refused to work at the current rates of wages. Fines were imposed upon a great number and variety of petty offenses, such as the new freemen were most likely to commit; and it was provided that, in the (extremely probable) event of the nonpayment of these fines, the culprits should be hired out to labor by judicial process. In some instances an elaborate system of compulsory apprenticeship was established for negroes under age, providing that they should be bound out to labor. In certain states the negroes were required to sign written contracts of labor, and were forbidden to do job work without first obtaining licenses from the police authorities of their places of residence. Those who failed to obtain licenses were liable to the charge of vagrancy, and upon that charge could be arrested, fined, and put to compulsory labor. There was not everywhere the same rigor; but there was everywhere the same determination to hold the negroes very watchfully, and, if need were, very sternly, within bounds in the exercise of their unaccustomed freedom; and in many cases the restraints imposed went the length of a veritable "involuntary servitude."

Congress had not waited to see these things done before attempting to help the negroes to make use of their freedom—and self-defensive use of it, at that. By an act of March 3, 1865, it established, as a branch of the War Department, a Bureau of Refugees, Freedmen, and Abandoned Lands, which was authorized and empowered to assist the one-time slaves in finding means of subsistence, and in making good their new privileges and immunities as citizens. The officials of this bureau, with the War Department behind them, had gone the whole length of extensive authority; putting away from the outset all ideas of accommodation, and preferring the interests of their wards to the interests of peaceable, wholesome, and healing progress. No doubt that was inevitable. What they did was but the final and direct application of the rigorous, unsentimental logic of events. The negroes, at any rate, had the full advantage of the federal power. A very active and officious branch of the War Department saw to it that the new disabilities which the southern legislatures sought to put upon them should as far as possible be rendered inoperative.

That, however, did not suffice to sweeten the temper of Congress. The fact remained that Mr. Johnson had rehabilitated the governments of the southern states without asking the leave of the houses; that the legislatures which he had authorized them to call together had sought, in the very same sessions in which they gave their assent to the emancipating amendment, virtually to undo the work of emancipation, substituting a slavery of legal restraints and disabilities for a slavery of private ownership; and that these same legislatures had sent men to Washington, to seek admission to the Senate, who were known, many of them, still openly to avow their unshaken belief in the right of secession. The southern voters, too, who had qualified by taking the oath prescribed by the President's proclamation, had in most instances sent men similarly unconvinced to ask admission to the House of Representatives. Here was indeed a surrender of all the advantages of the contest of arms, as it seemed to the radicals—very generous, no doubt, but done by a Tennesseean and a Democrat, who was evidently a little more than generous; done, too, to exalt the Executive above Congress; in any light, perilous and not to be tolerated. Even those who were not radicals wished that the restoration of the states, which all admitted to be necessary, had been effected in some other way, and safeguarded against this manifest error, as all deemed it, of putting the negroes back into the hands of those who had been their masters, and would not now willingly consent to be their fellow citizens.

Congress, accordingly, determined to take matters into its own hands. With the southern representatives excluded, there was a Republican majority in both houses strong enough to do what it pleased, even to the overriding, if necessary, of the President's vetoes. Upon assembling for their regular session in December, 1865, therefore, the House and Senate at once set up, by concurrent resolution, a joint committee of nine Representatives and six Senators, which was instructed to inquire into all the conditions obtaining in the southern states, and, after sufficient inquiry, advise the houses upon the question whether, under the governments which Mr. Johnson had given them, those states were entitled to representation. To this committee, in other words, was intrusted the whole guidance of Congress in the all-important and delicate business of the full rehabilitation of the southern states as members of the Union. By February, 1866, it had virtually been settled that the admission of their representatives to Congress should await the action of the reconstruction committee; and that purpose was very consistently adhered to. An exception was made in the case of Tennessee, but in her case only. The houses presently agreed to be satisfied with her "reconstruction," and admitted her representatives to their seats in both House and Senate by an act of the 24th of July, 1866. But the other states were put off until the joint committee had forced them through a process of "Thorough," which began their reconstruction at the very beginning, again, and executed at every stage the methods preferred by the houses. The leader throughout the drastic business was Mr. Thaddeus Stevens, of Pennsylvania, the chairman of the committee, the leader of the House. He was foremost among the radicals, and drew a following about him, much as Stephen Douglas had attached thoroughgoing Democrats to himself, in the old days when the legislative battles were being fought over the extension of slavery into the territories—by audacity, plain speaking, and the straightforward energy of unhesitating opinion. He gave directness and speed to all he proposed. He understood better than Douglas did the coarse work of hewing out practicable paths of action in the midst of opinions and interests at odds. He had no timidity, no

scruples about keeping to constitutional lines of policy, no regard or thought for the sensibilities of the minority—being
roughhewn and without embarrassing sensibilities himself—an
ideal radical for the service of the moment.

Careful men, trained in the older ways of statesmanship and
accustomed to reading the Constitution into all that they did,
tried to form some consistent theory of constitutional right with
regard to the way in which Congress ought to deal with this new
and unprecedented situation. The southern states were still
"states" within the meaning of the Constitution as the Supreme
Court had interpreted it. They were communities of free citizens; each had kept its territorial boundaries unchanged, unmistakable; in each there was an organized government, "sanctioned
and limited by a written constitution, and established by the
consent of the governed." Their officers of government, like
their people, had for a time, indeed, repudiated the authority of
the federal government; but they were now ready to acknow-
ledge that authority again, and could resume their normal relations with the other states at a moment's notice, with all proper
submission. Both Mr. Lincoln and Mr. Johnson had acted in part
upon these assumptions. They had objected only that the governments actually in existence at the close of the war had been
chosen by persons who were in fact insurgents, and that their
officers had served to organize rebellion. Let those citizens of the
South who had made submission, and who had been pardoned
under the President's proclamation, reconstitute their governments, repudiating their old leaders, and the only taint upon their
statehood would be removed: the Executive would recognize
them as again normally constituted members of the Union.

Not many members of Congress, however, accepted this view.
The Republican party, it was true, had entered upon the war
emphatically disavowing either wish or purpose to interfere
with the constitutional rights of the states; declaring its sole object to be the preservation of the Union—the denial of a single

particular right which it could not but view as revolutionary. But war had brought many things in its train. The heat and struggle of those four tremendous years had burned and scarred the body of affairs with many an ineffaceable fact, which could not now be overlooked. Legally or illegally, as states or as bodies of individuals merely, the southern people had been at war with the Union; the slaves had been freed by force of arms; their freedom had now been incorporated in the supreme law of the land, and must be made good to them; there was manifest danger that too liberal a theory of restoration would bring about an impossible tangle of principles, an intolerable contradiction between fact and fact. Mr. Sumner held that, by resisting the authority of the Union, of which they were members, the southern states had simply committed suicide, destroying their own institutions along with their allegiance to the federal government. They ceased to be states, he said, when they ceased to fulfill the duties imposed upon them by the fundamental law of the land. Others declined any such doctrine. They adhered, with an instinct almost of affection, to the idea of a veritable federal Union; rejected Mr. Sumner's presupposition that the states were only subordinate parts of a consolidated national government; and insisted that, whatever rights they had for a time forfeited, the southern states were at least not destroyed, but only estopped from exercising their ordinary functions within the Union, pending a readjustment.

Theories made Mr. Stevens very impatient. It made little difference with him whether the southern states had forfeited their rights by suicide, or temporary disorganization, or individual rebellion. As a matter of fact, every department of the federal government, the courts included, had declared the citizens of those states public enemies; the Constitution itself had been for four years practically laid aside, so far as they were concerned, as a document of peace; they had been overwhelmed by force, and were now held in subjection under military rule, like conquered provinces. It was just as well, he thought, to act upon the facts, and let theories alone. It was enough that all Congressmen were agreed—at any rate, all who were allowed a voice in the matter—that it was properly the part of Congress, and not of the Executive, to bring order out of the chaos: to see that federal supremacy and federal law were made good in the South; the legal changes brought about by the war forced upon its acceptance; and the negroes secured in the enjoyment of the equality and even the privileges of citizens, in accordance with the federal guarantee that there should be a republican form of government in every state—a government founded upon the consent of a majority of its adult subjects. The essential point was that Congress, the lawmaking power, should be in control. The President had been too easy to satisfy, too prompt, and too lenient. Mr. Stevens consented once and again that the language of fine-drawn theories of constitutional right should be used in the reports of the joint Committee on Reconstruction, in which he managed to be master; but the motto of the committee in all practical matters was his motto of "Thorough," and its policy made Congress supreme.

The year 1866 passed, with all things at sixes and sevens. So far as the President was concerned, most of the southern states were already reconstructed, and had resumed their places in the Union. Their assent had made the Thirteenth Amendment a part of the Constitution. And yet Congress forbade the withdrawal of the troops, refused admittance to the southern representatives, and set aside southern laws through the action of the Freedmen's Bureau and the military authorities. By 1867 it had made up its mind what to do to bring the business to a conclusion. 1866 had at least cleared its mind and defined its purposes. Congress had still further tested and made proof of the temper of the South. In June it had adopted a Fourteenth Amendment, which secured to the blacks the status of citizens, both of the United States and of the several states of their residence, authorized a reduction in the representation in Congress of states which refused them the suffrage, excluded the more prominent servants of the Confederacy from federal office until Congress should pardon them, and invalidated all debts or obligations "incurred in aid of insurrection or rebellion against the United States"; and this amendment had been submitted to the vote of the states which Congress had refused to recognize as well as to the vote of those represented in the houses. Tennessee had promptly adopted it, and had been as promptly admitted to representation. But the other southern states, as promptly as they could, had begun, one by one, to reject it. Their action confirmed the houses in their attitude toward Reconstruction.

Congressional views and purposes were cleared the while with regard to the President, also. He had not been firm; he had been stubborn and bitter. He would yield nothing; vetoed the measures upon which Congress was most steadfastly minded to insist; alienated his very friends by attacking Congress in public with gross insult and abuse; and lost credit with everybody. It came to a direct issue, the President against Congress: they went to the country with their quarrel in the congressional elections, which fell opportunely in the autumn of 1866, and the President lost utterly. Until then some had hesitated to override his vetoes, but after that no one hesitated. 1867 saw Congress go triumphantly forward with its policy of reconstruction *ab initio.*

In July, 1866, it had overridden a veto to continue and enlarge the powers of the Freedmen's Bureau, in a bill which directed that public lands should be sold to the negroes upon easy terms, that the property of the Confederate government should be appropriated for their education, and that their new-made rights should be protected by military authority. In March, 1867, two acts, passed over the President's vetoes, instituted the new process of reconstruction, followed and completed by another act in July of the same year. The southern states, with the exception, of course, of Tennessee, were grouped in five military districts,

each of which was put under the command of a general of the
United States. These commanders were made practically absolute rulers, until the task of reconstruction should be ended. It
was declared by the Reconstruction Acts that no other legal
state governments existed in the ten states concerned. It was
made the business of the district commanders to erect such governments as Congress prescribed. They were to enroll in each
state, upon oath, all male citizens of one year's residence, not dis-
qualified by reason of felony or excluded under the terms of the
proposed Fourteenth Amendment, "of whatever race, color, or
previous condition" they might be; the persons thus registered
were to choose constitutional conventions, confining their
choice of delegates to registered voters like themselves; these
conventions were to be directed to frame state constitutions,
which should extend the suffrage to all who had been permitted
by the military authorities to enroll for the purpose of taking
part in the election of delegates; and the constitutions were to
be submitted to the same body of voters for ratification. When
Congress had approved the constitutions thus framed and accepted, and when the legislatures constituted under them had
adopted the Fourteenth Amendment, the states thus reorganized
were to be readmitted to representation in Congress, and in all
respects fully reinstated as members of the Union; but not before. Meanwhile, the civil governments already existing within
them, though illegal, were to be permitted to stand; but as "provisional only, and in all respects subject to the paramount authority of the United States at any time to abolish, control, or
supersede the same."

Such was the process which was rigorously and consistently
carried through during the memorable years 1867–70; and upon
the states which proved most difficult and recalcitrant Congress
did not hesitate from time to time to impose new conditions of
recognition and reinstatement before an end was made. By the
close of July, 1868, the reconstruction and reinstatement of Ar-

kansas, the two Carolinas, Florida, Alabama, and Louisiana had been completed. Virginia, Mississippi, and Texas were obliged to wait until the opening of 1870, because their voters would not adopt the constitutions offered them by their reconstructing conventions; and Georgia was held off a few months longer, because she persisted in attempting to exclude negroes from the right to hold office. These four states, as a consequence, were obliged to accept, as a condition precedent to their reinstatement, not only the Fourteenth Amendment, but a Fifteenth also, which Congress had passed in February, 1869, and which forbade either the United States or any state to withhold from any citizen the right to vote "on account of race, color, or previous condition of servitude." The military commanders, meanwhile, used or withheld their hand of power according to their several temperaments. They could deal with the provisional civil governments as they pleased—could remove officials, annul laws, regulate administration, at will. Some were dictatorial and petty; some were temperate and guarded in their use of authority, with a creditable instinct of statesmanship; almost all were straightforward and executive, as might have been expected of soldiers.

Whatever their mistakes or weaknesses of temper or of judgment, what followed the reconstruction they effected was in almost every instance much worse than what had had to be endured under miltary rule. The first practical result of reconstruction under the acts of 1867 was the disfranchisement, for several weary years, of the better whites, and the consequent giving over of the southern governments into the hands of the negroes. And yet not into their hands, after all. They were but children still; and unscrupulous men, "carpetbaggers"—men not come to be citizens, but come upon an expedition of profit, come to make the name of Republican forever hateful in the South— came out of the North to use the negroes as tools for their own selfish ends; and succeeded, to the utmost fulfillment of their dreams. Negro majorities for a little while filled the southern

legislatures; but they won no power or profit for themselves, beyond a pittance here and there for a bribe. Their leaders, strangers and adventurers, got the lucrative offices, the handling of the
state moneys raised by loan, and of the taxes spent no one knew
how. Here and there an able and upright man cleansed administration, checked corruption, served them as a real friend and
an honest leader; but not for long. The negroes were exalted; the
states were misgoverned and looted in their name; and a few
men, not of their number, not really of their interest, went away
with the gains. They were left to carry the discredit and reap
the consequences of ruin, when at last the whites who were real
citizens got control again.

But that dark chapter of history is no part of our present story.
We are here concerned, rather, with the far-reaching constitutional and political influences and results of reconstruction. That
it was a revolutionary process is written upon its face throughout; but how deep did the revolution go? What permanent
marks has it left upon the great structure of government, federal,
republican; a partnership of equal states, and yet a solidly coher-
ent national power, which the fathers erected?

First of all, it is clear to every one who looks straight upon the
facts, every veil of theory withdrawn, and the naked body of
affairs uncovered to meet the direct question of the eye, that
civil war discovered the foundations of our government to be in
fact unwritten; set deep in a sentiment which constitutions can
neither originate nor limit. The law of the Constitution reigned
until war came. Then the stage was cleared, and the forces of a
mighty sentiment, hitherto unorganized, deployed upon it. A
thing had happened for which the Constitution had made no
provision. In the Constitution were written the rules by which
the associated states should live in concert and union, with no
word added touching days of discord or disruption; nothing
about the use of force to keep or to break the authority ordained
in its quiet sentences, written, it would seem, for lawyers, not for

soldiers. When the war came, therefore, and questions were broached to which it gave no answer, the ultimate foundation of the structure was laid bare; physical force, sustained by the stern loves and rooted predilections of masses of men, the strong ingrained prejudices which are the fibre of every system of government. What gave the war its passion, its hot energy as of a tragedy from end to end, was that in it sentiment met sentiment, conviction, conviction. It was the sentiment, not of all, but of the efficient majority, the conviction of the major part, that won. A minority, eager and absolute in another conviction, devoted to the utmost pitch of self-sacrifice to an opposite and incompatible ideal, was crushed and overwhelmed. It was that which gave an epic breadth and majesty to the awful clash between bodies of men in all things else of one strain and breeding; it was that which brought the bitterness of death upon the side which lost, and the dangerous intoxication of an absolute triumph upon the side which won. But it unmistakably uncovered the foundations of force upon which the Union rested.

It did more. The sentiment of union and nationality, never before aroused to full consciousness or knowledge of its own thought and aspirations, was henceforth a new thing, aggressive and aware of a sort of conquest. It had seen its legions and felt its might in the field. It saw the very Constitution, for whose maintenance and defense it had acquired the discipline of arms, itself subordinated for a time to the practical emergencies of war, in order that the triumph might be the more unimpeded and complete; and it naturally deemed nationality henceforth a thing above law. As much as possible—so far as could be without serious embarrassment—the forms of the fundamental law had indeed been respected and observed; but wherever the law clogged or did not suffice, it had been laid aside and ignored. It was so much the easier, therefore, to heed its restrictions lightly, when the war was over, and it became necessary to force the southern states to accept the new model. The real revolution was not so

much in the form as in the spirit of affairs. The spirit and temper
and method of a federal Union had given place, now that all the
spaces of the air had been swept and changed by the merciless
winds of war, to a spirit which was consciously national and of a
new age.

It was this spirit which brushed theories and technicalities
aside, and impressed its touch of revolution on the law itself. And
not only upon the law, but also upon the processes of lawmaking, and upon the relative positions of the President and Congress in the general constitutional scheme of the government,
seeming to change its very administrative structure. While the
war lasted the President had been master; the war ended, and Mr.
Lincoln gone, Congress pushed its way to the front, and began
to transmute fact into law, law into fact. In some matters it
treated all the states alike. The Thirteenth, Fourteenth, and Fifteenth amendments bound all the states at once, North and West
as well as South. But that was, after all, a mere equality of form.
The amendments were aimed, of course, at the states which had
had slaves and had attempted secession, and did not materially
affect any others. The votes which incorporated them in the
Constitution were voluntary on the part of the states whose institutions they did not affect, involuntary on the part of the
states whose institutions they revolutionized. These states were
then under military rule. Congress had declared their whole political organization to be illegal; had excluded their representatives from their seats in the houses; and yet demanded that they
assent, as states, to the amendment of the Constitution as a condition precedent to their reinstatement in the Union! No ano-
maly or contradiction of lawyers' terms was suffered to stand in
the way of the supremacy of the lawmaking branch of the general government. The Constitution knew no such process as this
of reconstruction, and could furnish no rules for it. Two years
and a half before the Fifteenth Amendment was adopted by
Congress, three years and a half before it was put in force by its

adoption by the states, Congress had by mere act forced the southern states, by the hands of military governors, to put the negroes upon the roll of their voters. It had dictated to them a radical revision of their constitutions, whose items should be framed to meet the views of the houses rather than the views of their own electors. It had pulled about and rearranged what local institutions it saw fit, and then had obliged the communities affected to accept its alterations as the price of their reinstatement as self-governing bodies politic within the Union.

It may be that much, if not all, of this would have been inevitable under any leadership, the temper of the times and the posture of affairs being what they were; and it is certain that it was inevitable under the actual circumstances of leadership then existing at Washington. But to assess that matter is to reckon with causes. For the moment we are concerned only with consequences, and are neither justifying nor condemning, but only comprehending. The courts of the United States have held that the southern states never were out of the Union; and yet they have justified the action of Congress throughout the process of reconstruction, on the ground that it was no more than a proper performance by Congress of a legal duty, under the clause of the Constitution which guarantees to every state a republican form of government. It was making the southern governments republican by securing full standing and legislative representation as citizens for the negroes. But Congress went beyond that. It not only dictated to the states it was reconstructing what their suffrage should be; it also required that they should never afterward narrow that suffrage. It required of Virginia, Texas, and Mississippi that they should accord to the negroes not only the right to vote, but also the right to hold political office; and that they should grant to all their citizens equal school privileges, and never afterward abridge them. So far as the right to vote was concerned, the Fifteenth Amendment subsequently imposed the same disability with regard to withholding the suffrage upon all the states alike; but the southern states were also forbidden by mere federal statute to restrict it on any other ground; and in the cases of Virginia, Mississippi, and Texas Congress assumed the right, which the Constitution nowhere accorded it, to regulate admission to political office and the privileges of public education.

South Carolina and Mississippi, Louisiana and North Carolina, have since changed the basis of their suffrage, notwithstanding; Virginia and Mississippi and Texas might now, no doubt, reorganize their educational system as they pleased, without endangering their status in the Union, or even meeting rebuke at the hands of the federal courts. The temper of the times has changed; the federal structure has settled to a normal balance of parts and functions again; and the states are in fact unfettered except by the terms of the Constitution itself. It is marvelous what healing and oblivion peace has wrought, how the traces of reconstruction have worn away. But a certain deep effect abides. It is within, not upon the surface. It is of the spirit, not of the body. A revolution was carried through when war was done which may be better comprehended if likened to England's subtle making over, that memorable year 1688. Though she punctiliously kept to the forms of her law, England then dismissed a king almost as, in later years, she would have dismissed a minister; though she preserved the procedure of her constitution intact, she in fact gave a final touch of change to its spirit. She struck irresponsible power away, and made her government once for all a constitutional government. The change had been insensibly a-making for many a long age; but now it was accomplished consciously and at a stroke. Her constitution, finished, was not what it had been until this stroke was given—when silent forces had at last found sudden voice, and the culminating change was deliberately made.

Nearly the same can be said of the effect of the war and of the reconstruction of the southern states upon our own government.

It was a revolution of consciousness—of mind and purpose. A government which had been in its spirit federal became, almost of a sudden, national in temper and point of view. The national spirit had long been a-making. Many a silent force, which grew quite unobserved, from generation to generation, in pervasiveness and might, in quiet times of wholesome peace and mere increase of nature, had been breeding these thoughts which now sprang so vividly into consciousness. The very growth of the nation, the very lapse of time and uninterrupted habit of united action, the mere mixture and movement and distribution of populations, the mere accretions of policy, the mere consolidation of interests, had been building and strengthening new tissue of nationality the years through, and drawing links stronger than links of steel round about the invisible body of common thought and purpose which is the substance of nations. When the great crisis of secession came, men knew at once how their spirits were ruled, men of the South as well as men of the North—in what institutions and conceptions of government their blood was fixed to run; and a great and instant readjustment took place, which was for the South, the minority, practically the readjustment of conquest and fundamental reconstruction, but which was for the North, the region which had been transformed, nothing more than an awakening.

It cannot be said that the forms of the Constitution were observed in this quick change as the forms of the English constitution had been observed when the Stuarts were finally shown the door. There were no forms for such a business. For several years, therefore, Congress was permitted to do by statute what, under the long-practiced conception of our federal law, could properly be done only by constitutional amendment. The necessity for that gone by, it was suffered to embody what it had already enacted and put into force as law into the Constitution, not by the free will of the country at large, but by the compulsions of mere force exercised upon a minority whose assent was necessary to the formal completion of its policy. The result restored, practically entire, the forms of the Constitution; but not before new methods and irregular, the methods of majorities, but not the methods of law, had been openly learned and practiced, and learned in a way not likely to be forgot. Changes of law in the end gave authentic body to many of the most significant changes of thought which had come, with its new consciousness, to the nation. A citizenship of the United States was created; additional private civil rights were taken within the jurisdiction of the general government; additional prohibitions were put upon the states; the suffrage was in a measure made subject to national regulation. But the real change was the change of air—a change of conception with regard to the power of Congress, the guiding and compulsive efficacy of national legislation, the relation of the life of the land to the supremacy of the national lawmaking body. All policy thenceforth wore a different aspect.

We realize it now, in the presence of novel enterprises, at the threshold of an unlooked-for future. It is evident that empire is an affair of strong government, and not of the nice and somewhat artificial poise or of the delicate compromises of structure and authority characteristic of a mere federal partnership. Undoubtedly, the impulse of expansion is the natural and wholesome impulse which comes with a consciousness of matured strength; but it is also a direct result of that national spirit which the war between the states cried so wide awake, and to which the processes of reconstruction gave the subtle assurance of practically unimpeded sway and a free choice of means. The revolution lies there, as natural as it was remarkable and full of prophecy. It is this which makes the whole period of Reconstruction so peculiarly worthy of our study. Every step of the policy, every feature of the time, which wrought this subtle transformation, should receive our careful scrutiny. We are now far enough removed from the time to make that scrutiny both close and dispassionate. A new age gives it a new significance.

The Conditions of the Reconstruction Problem

HILARY A. HERBERT

Conditions in the late Confederate states, from "the surrender," as it is still called in the South, up to the passage of the act of March 2, 1867, overthrowing the Johnson governments, and establishing the congressional plan of reconstruction, were pathetic in the extreme.

Out of a white population of about five million, there had gone into the Confederate army six hundred and twenty-five thousand, and of these two hundred thousand had lost their lives. Many thousands more had been maimed. Many other thousands had enlisted in the armies of the Union, and they also had suffered severely.

Prussia was in a piteous plight at the close of the Seven Years' War, and so was France at the end of her great Revolution. But Prussia, after her direful disasters, still had a certain amount of currency, and had no debts; France was left deeply in debt, but she had her currency and her financial institutions; whereas the Confederates, whose bank notes were now worthless, and whose currency and bonds were left without any government behind them, had practically nothing to show for their past savings. There was this further difference: neither Prussia nor France had ever been cursed with slavery; and all the other misfortunes of the South, aggregated, were but fleeting and temporary when compared with the enduring problems, economic and political, which were to come from the sudden manumission of four millions of slaves.

Desolation had followed in the wake of armies. Plough stock had been taken, cattle and provisions consumed, fences destroyed, in places even cotton seed was not to be had; and almost no one had credit, where credit had once been nearly universal. The harvest of death had left nothing but debts and lands, and many landowners were without a dollar that would pay taxes, state or federal. Already in the Union for purposes of taxation, but still out of it politically, the people of the late Confederate states were at once to assume their full share of the debt of nearly three billions of dollars contracted in subjugating them; they were to pay also their share of the pensions to Union soldiers: and the money thus drained from the South, to be expended in the North during the coming thirty-five years, was to be far more than equal to all the expenses of the Southern state governments, including school funds and interest on state debts. The spring of 1865 witnessed indeed the completion of the transfer of wealth in the United States from the home of the Southern planter, where it was once supposed to exist, to the Northern section of the Union.

There was but one resource left. "King Cotton," during the past four years, had grievously disappointed the prophets who had boasted of his prowess; but now he came out from his hiding places, and showed that, though he could not as a sovereign turn the tide of unsuccessful war, he still could play the part of Santa Claus in time of peace. Never were children more delighted by the gray-bearded king of Christmas than were the helpless and hapless people of the South by the blessings that came to them from the fleecy staple—absolutely the only relief in sight. The cotton that had in war escaped Federal and Confederate torches, and that could elude the United States government agents, who were seizing it upon the plea, often groundless, that it had been subscribed to the Confederacy, brought high prices; and the money thus received, though wholly insufficient, was invaluable. It passed rapidly from hand to hand; for lessons of economy that are learned under compulsion are seldom taken to heart. Most of those who got money for cotton were in a mood for self-indulgence; they must put away the memory of the bitter past, and reward themselves for the sacrifices they had made. Women who had woven and worn homespuns, those who had cut up and sent their carpets to soldiers for blankets, must have silks and satins. Sorghum syrup, substitutes for coffee, and other economic makeshifts were relegated as far as possible to the limbo of the unhappy past.

These were the conditions that awaited the Confederate soldier at home. To appreciate his attitude, it must be recalled that as nine tenths of the Union army had enlisted to save the Union, and would have refused to join in a war having for its sole purpose the abolition of slavery, so five sixths of the Confederates were non-slaveholders, and had fought, not for slavery, but to maintain the old Constitution under an independent government. When it became apparent that independence was impossible, the war ended suddenly. There was no guerrilla warfare, prompted by hatred, as in South Africa or in the Philippines. The issue was decided, and the Confederate soldier turned his footsteps homeward, not ashamed of his defeat, but exulting in the thought that he could call upon mankind to witness he had made a brave fight. His cause was lost and his country desolated, but "hope springs eternal in the human breast." Now that slavery and secession were out of the way, he hoped for peace and prosperity in the old Union. One of the most notable features of his home-coming was the strangely intermingled gayety and gloom that everywhere, for weeks and months, pervaded society. The comrade who was never to return had met a soldier's fate; for him the tear had fallen as he was buried. Why should not the survivor be happy at meeting again those whom he had often thought he was nevermore to see? Mother, sister, wife, or sweetheart greeted him with joy, and as a hero who had deserved, if he did not achieve, success; and never were there gayer routs, dancing parties, and weddings than those which were everywhere witnessed throughout the late Confederacy in the times of which we write. Tables were often thinly spread, but youth and beauty and valor had shaken hands, the long agony of war was over, and the white dove of peace had come again. The theory of Malthus, that after devastating wars population increases with a bound, was being illustrated afresh. Marriages were more frequent than ever. Around camp fires and in lonely prison cells, the soldier, often a bachelor who had never before thought to prove Benedict, had been dreaming of a peaceful home, made happy by the smiles of wife and the prattle of children; and now, whatever else was in store for him, this dream must be realized.

But if the sunshine was strangely bright for some, others were in deepest gloom. Always in sight of the merrymaking that was so common were homes that were wrecked forever—husbands, fathers, sons, brothers, and fortunes, gone; and it was a matter of common remark that never had the mortality among persons who had passed middle age been so great in the late Confederate states as within the decade following 1865. Everywhere, men and women, brooding over the past, sank brokenhearted into their graves.

Its terrible losses and stinging defeat had naturally caused throughout the South much bitterness toward the North. This is well illustrated by the anecdote of the Virginian whose wife told him, one bright morning, that every negro had left the place; that he must cut the wood, and she must get breakfast. It is not recorded that the wife indulged in any expletives; but the husband, with the first stroke of the axe, damned "old Abe Lincoln for freeing the negroes"; with the next he went further back, and doubled-damned George Washington for setting up the United States Government; and with the third, going back to the first cause of all his woes, he double-double-damned Christopher Columbus for discovering America!

This feeling of vindictiveness, while it pervaded more or less all classes who had sympathized with the Confederacy, was far more intense among non-combatants than with the returned soldiers. These had learned to respect their foes. Courage had been demonstrated to be common to both armies; kind offices to the wounded and the hungry had been mutual, and the dividing of rations by Grant's veterans with Lee's at Appomattox was just what had occurred on a smaller scale many times before. But the non-combatants at the South (and so it must have been at the North, judging from subsequent events) had none of the kindly feelings with which soldiers regarded their adversaries. It was quite common in 1865 to hear a soldier say that, for himself, he had had "enough of it; but my neighbor, who has been hiding all the time at home behind a bombproof position, has just now begun to get mad. What a pity he couldn't have gotten his courage up before the fighting was over!" And now, thirty-five years afterwards, it may be affirmed without reserve that if the soldiers of the two armies had been allowed of themselves, uninfluenced by politicians, to dictate the terms of reconstruction, the history of the United States during the past three decades would have been widely different.

An added cause of bitterness among ex-Confederates was the imprisonment of Jefferson Davis, and his treatment in a manner that to the South seemed cruel and without justification. This generation has almost forgotten that, although Mr. Davis, then in feeble health, was doubly safe by reason of the strong casemate at Fortress Monroe and the guards that surrounded him, an officer was required to see him every fifteen minutes, day and night, thus breaking his rest; and that the prisoner was for a long time forbidden books, except the Bible, and all correspondence, even with his wife. Irons were at one time placed on his legs; but though these were soon removed, the condition of the captive, as reported by the post surgeon, caused in May, 1866, a vigorous protest not only in the South, but in prominent Northern journals. Those were days of intense excitement, even in the North. Naturally, the ex-Confederates looked upon their President as suffering for them, and were much embittered by this incident.

But the North was not always held responsible as the *fons et origo* of Southern misfortunes in those days, which were so full of gloom to all who took time to consider the conditions that surrounded them. There was a widespread feeling that the secession leaders were answerable for the calamitous situation. Many Whigs retained their old-time prejudices against Democrats, and in every Southern state there had been Unionists. These were disposed to claim the benefit of their superior judgment, and many indeed were now "Union men" whose Union sentiments prior to secession their friends were by no means able to recall.

The disposition to put down the secessionists had received a powerful impulse from an unfortunate and unwise law passed by the Confederate Congress, exempting from service in the army, under certain conditions, the owners of twenty negroes, on the ground that they were needed at home to raise food-stuffs. Even in the army it had been bruited about, "This is the rich man's war, and the poor man's fight." In most of the states, the feeling of comradeship among Confederate soldiers would have rendered improbable any very equal division at the outset between secessionists and anti-secessionists; but certain it is that here were lines of cleavage that would inevitably have divided the Southern people into two bitterly hostile factions, had not the sempiternal negro question now appeared again, and this time in a form that was eventually to bring about a greater solidarity, even, than had come from the invasion of Northern armies. The shape it assumed was the suffrage involved in the reconstruction problem.

If the condition of the Southern white in 1865–66 was such as to command, from the present standpoint, the sympathy of the generous-minded, still more strikingly pitiful and helpless was the condition of the freedman. Not in all the imaginings of the Arabian Nights is there any concept so startling as the sudden manumission of four millions of slaves, left unshackled to shift for themselves—without property, without resources excepting their labor, without mental training, and with no traditions save only such as connected them with bondage and barbarism. What was to become of these people? Would their energies be properly directed, and would they, as other peoples had done, gradually build up with their strong arms a future for themselves? Or would they be misdirected and led away from reliance on labor into fields where, by reason of their limitations, success was impossible? This was not for the freedman to decide. It was a problem for the white man, the Caucasian, who makes and unmakes the laws and governments of the world; who fashions civilizations, sometimes in comely shape, sometimes awry, but always in moulds of his own making. And it was still further a question as to what white man was to undertake the solution of this problem. Was it to be the white man whose lot was cast in the same land with the freedman, or was it to be the man who sympathized with him from afar, but knew him not?

Rehabilitation of the states, therefore, involving as it did the future relations of both whites and blacks to the states and the federal government, marked a crisis in our history second in import only to that created by the attempt to secede. The task was delicate, and called for deliberation and wise statesmanship. If, instead, the intense patriotism and philanthropy of the hour were allowed to become only the handmaids of acrimony and political ardor, and if results have proven the policy adopted to

have been fraught with evil, the commentator fails of his duty
who does not set up a beacon light to warn his countrymen of
the dangers that come to the ship of state from venturing, when
full-freighted, into the stormy waters of partisanship; for assuredly the perils of the future are not to be avoided by conceal-
ing or glossing over either the errors of the past or the reasoning
upon which they proceeded.

Mr. Lincoln, as early as December 8, 1863, had formulated a
plan of reconstruction by the Executive—voters to be those who
were qualified "by the election laws of the state, existing immediately before the so-called act of secession, and excluding all
others"; but Congress had afterwards passed a joint resolution asserting its own power over reconstruction. Mr. Lincoln, it is
true, killed this resolution by a pocket veto; but the great head
of his party had been removed by an assassin, and there stood the
action of Congress, and the declaration of Mr. Sumner, one of its
foremost leaders, on the 25th of February, 1865, that "the cause
of human rights and of the Union needed the ballots as well as
the muskets of colored men."

It was feared in the South that President Johnson, especially
after he had said that traitors must be deprived of social position,
and "treason made odious," would share Mr. Sumner's views.
Mr. Sumner has claimed that for a time he did; but if so, the
President soon changed his mind, for on the 9th of May, 1865,
he made an order recognizing Mr. Lincoln's plan in Virginia, and
on May 29 he issued his proclamation for the reconstruction of
North Carolina, excluding negroes, and recognizing as voters
only those qualified by the state law at the date of the attempt to
secede.

The continued presence of the military and the aggravating
conduct of many of the officials of the Freedmen's Bureau were
causing much dissatisfaction at the time of this proclamation; yet
it was an immeasurable relief to feel that the seceded states were

to be admitted without putting the ballot into the hands of the ex-slave.

The repugnance of Southern white men to negro suffrage was extreme. Edmund Burke, in one of his speeches in the British Parliament, pointing out the difficulties in the way of the subjugation of the American colonies, explained that in all the slave-holding communities there was an aristocracy of color; every white man felt himself to belong to a superior race, and this pride of race to an extent ennobled and elevated him. It was a true picture, and such a people were naturally prejudiced against meeting their inferior, the negro, as an equal at the ballot box. But their aversion had a better foundation than prejudice. The negro had nowhere shown himself capable of self-government. White manhood suffrage had obtained for years in all the seceded states, and never had the suffrage been purer or given better results. The population was largely of English and Scotch descent. Free schools had not been general, and illiteracy was more prevalent than in the Northern states; but joint discussions before the people by candidates for office were almost universal, while the code of honor regulating duels, then sanctioned by public opinion, exacted from every speaker rigid responsibility for his statements in debate; and so it came about that even among those who were uneducated there were unusually correct ideas of the high duties discharged by freemen in casting their ballots. Their suffrages were not for sale, and in self-government the morality and patriotism of voters count for almost everything; without these, booklearning is a snare.

It is easy enough to write that the success of universal manhood suffrage for whites, although in evidence both North and South, was not a sufficient argument for giving the ballot to every male over twenty-one among four millions of ex-slaves, and to add that a question like this ought to have been decided on its merits, and without regard to its effects on political parties

This is a truth that was recognized by Mr. Lincoln and by Mr. Johnson, each feeling that the burden of decision rested upon him. Individual responsibility sobers and lifts men up to meet great crises. Divided authority, however, weakens the sense of responsibility, and leaves passion full play, especially in a numerous body like Congress; and never was there so much bitterness between parties, or so much at stake upon the action of Congress. The Confederacy, after a bloody war against the Union, was prostrate. Should ex-Confederates come back with increased membership in Congress, representing all the negroes as freedmen, instead of, as previously, three fifths of the negroes as slaves? Should the party claiming to be the party of the Union incur the danger of handing over the government to an alliance of ex-Confederates with the Democrats, who in their platform of 1864 had denounced the war for the Union as a failure? Had not the North freed the slave? Was not this freedman the ward of the nation? Ought not the government to be keenly watchful of his interests, and was it not a duty to protect him and give him power to protect himself? The ballot was clearly the remedy, provided the freedman was competent to wield it. This was the question—competency—and it called for decision on its own merits; but passion, prejudice, love of power, philanthropy, and a sense of justice to the negro, all combined to obscure the issue, and to make it, as it soon became in Congress, a party question. A few Republicans were to oppose their party in the House and Senate, and be soon driven out of public life. The party that elected Mr. Johnson was to oppose him, and the party that opposed him in the election was to sustain him unanimously in Congress. This President, who had come to his office on account of his services to the Union, was to become the best friend, the adviser, and the leader of the ex-Confederates in a political contest; and occupying this peculiar attitude, he had uncommon need of tact, in which, unfortunately for his new allies, he was singularly lacking.

The Southern whites looked upon negro suffrage as a crime

against Republican government—a crime against which the people of the North, and if not they, then the President and the Supreme Court, would protect them. They had abandoned in good faith both slavery and secession, all that they thought were in issue, and now they were uncompromising in demanding what they denominated their "rights" as conceded by Lincoln and by Johnson. They never once thought of a compromise, but staked all upon the result of the fight between the President and Congress.

From March 4 till December 4, 1865, Congress was not in session, and during all this time Mr. Johnson was busy carrying out in the Southern states Mr. Lincoln's plan of reconstruction. The result was that when Congress convened, in December, Representatives and Senators from most of the late Confederate states were applying for admission. The Thirteenth Amendment, abolishing slavery, had been ratified by these states, and new constitutions had been adopted. The issue was thus fairly presented—whether Congress would recognize reconstruction after the Lincoln-Johnson plan. The new constitutions set up under Johnson all confined suffrage to white men.

It is strange that, inasmuch as the country was yet to pass upon the question, Mr. Johnson, in his message in December, 1865, and elsewhere in his many public utterances, should not have appealed earnestly for support to the memory of his great predecessor, the author of the plan he was pursuing. On the contrary, prompted probably by egotism, he always spoke of the policy as his own.

It has been said that Mr. Lincoln's Southern birth and association with Southern men naturally inclined him against negro suffrage. Johnson was not only born in the South, but had always lived there. The views of the two Presidents as to who ought to exercise the power to define suffrage, and as to the manner in which that power should be exerted by the Southern states, were almost identical.

Mr. Lincoln wrote to Governor Hahn, when the convention

he had called to reconstruct Louisiana during the war was about to assemble: "I barely suggest for your private consideration whether some of the colored people may not be let in, as, for instance, the very intelligent, and especially those who have fought gallantly in our ranks." So Mr. Johnson, August 15, 1865, to Governor Sharkey, of Mississippi: "If you could extend the elective franchise to all persons of color who can read and write, and who have a certain amount of property, etc., you would *completely disarm the adversary*, and set an example that other states would follow."

It would have been wise for Mississippi and the other Southern states to follow the advice given Governor Sharkey. The few negroes qualified under these restrictions could have done no harm, and such a course might have had weight with voters in the North, to whom the general policy Congress was pursuing toward the South was to be submitted before the venture upon negro suffrage was made.

The majority sentiment in Congress did not, at the outset, favor negro suffrage as a condition of rehabilitation, and progress in that direction was not rapid. In the spring of 1865, the New York *Tribune*, while contending that the negro was entitled to the ballot, was urging the unwisdom of taking issue with a Republican President who had at hand all the patronage of the government. When, however, the 4th of July, the national anniversary, had come, orations were made by such leaders as Boutwell in Massachusetts, Garfield in Ohio, and Julian in Indiana, advocating broadly negro suffrage for the late Confederate states,—and this before a single state convention had assembled under Johnson's reconstruction proclamations.

In forwarding the claim of the negro for the ballot no factor was more powerful than the Freedmen's Bureau. The Bureau had been established by the act of March 3, 1865, to take care of the freedmen who were flocking into the Union lines; and as those lines advanced the Bureau had been extended all over the

South. Backed by the bayonet, and exercising absolute power to settle disputes between two races where natural friction was easily aggravated, the officers of the Bureau had exceptional opportunities for good or for evil. Many performed their duties faithfully; but many others were in search even then of the offices that were afterwards to come by the votes of their wards. To get these offices, the North must be made to believe that the ballot was a necessity for the negro; and it was easy, especially for the subordinate officials who dealt directly with the freedman, to encourage discontent among their wards and strife between the races. The Southern white man was frequently impulsive, and, when vexed by negro "insolence" and by the stories that came to him of the injustice at Bureau headquarters, where often, in negro language, "the bottom rail was on top," he took justice into his own hands, and sometimes it was injustice. Race prejudice was also here and there painfully apparent in superior courts and in juries. Thus there was enough truth in some of the many stories of outrages that were circulated in the North to make them all current at their face value. So it came about that the Freedmen's Bureau, the real purpose of which was to make contracts for the freedmen, settle questions between them and their employers, and take care of its wards generally, was, through many dishonest and partisan officials who were attached to it, proving to be a prime factor in the manufacture of political opinion during the whole period covered by this article. The reports of Bureau chiefs, where they spoke of quiet, passed unnoticed; it was the reports of outrages that attracted attention.

The dispensing of supplies without price to able-bodied persons must always tend to produce idleness: this tendency of its own work it was the especial duty of the Freedmen's Bureau to correct. The greatest crisis that had ever occurred in the lives of four million people had arrived. Slavery had lifted the Southern negro to a plane of civilization never before attained by any large body of his race—had taught him to be law-abiding and industrious. If the guardians of this man, who was bewildered by his new surroundings, and who was clay, though unwashed clay, in the hands of the potter, had shown him the absolute necessity of continued industry, the negro would have had at this critical moment the best chance of thrift that was ever to come to him. But, unluckily, this was not to be. Instead of being properly directed, the credulous freedman was in many instances encouraged in idleness, while he was deluded by false hopes. General Grant, in a report to the President, after having made a tour of inspection in the South, though he qualified his statement by attributing to "many, and perhaps a majority of them," the inculcation of proper ideas, nevertheless said, "The belief widely spread among the freedmen of the Southern states, that the lands of the former owners will at least in part be divided among them, has come from the agents of this Bureau;" and further, "The effect of the belief in the division of lands is idleness and accumulation in towns and cities."

Idleness is the prolific parent of hunger, want, and crime, and the widespread idleness prevailing everywhere in the South in the fall and winter of 1865 called loudly for legislation. It was during this period that the legislatures elected under the presidential reconstruction plan were in session, and passed, most of them, vagrancy and apprenticeship laws, some containing very stringent provisions. These statutes embraced, most of them without material variations, the features of the old law of Maine, brought forward in Rev. Stats. of 1883, sec. 17, p. 925, providing that one who goes about begging, etc., "shall be deemed a tramp, and be imprisoned at hard labor," etc.; and the old law of Rhode Island, brought forward in Rev. Stats. of 1872, p. 243, "If any servant or apprentice shall depart from the service of his master or otherwise neglect his duty," he may be committed to the workhouse; and the long-existing law of Connecticut, contained in the Revision of 1866, p. 320, punishing by fine or imprisonment one who shall entice a "minor [apprentice] from the service or employment of such master."

In some instances details were harsher than in the New England laws, but existing conditions were without precedent. Southern legislators were excited by the aggravated evils that surrounded them, and they seem never to have thought of political results.

One feature that was in practically all these apprentice laws, and that attracted general attention at the North, was a provision giving preference as masters to former owners of negro minors when before a court to be bound over. This was looked upon by many Northern voters as conclusive evidence of an intent to continue slavery, as far as could be, exactly as it had existed. In reality it was a humane provision. William H. Council, Booker T. Washington, and other leading colored students of the negro question, as it has been bequeathed to us from the days of Reconstruction, concur in holding that the negro's best friend at the South was and is the former slaveholder. But, unfortunately, Southern legislators did not know that here they were outraging the sympathies of Northern voters.

The features of this legislation that met with the most universal condemnation were the Mississippi law of November 25, 1865, requiring every freedman to make a contract for a home and work by the second Monday in January, 1866; a similar law of Louisiana, passed in December; and a statute of Mississippi, punishing unlawful assemblages of blacks, or of whites and blacks mixed. Acts were also passed by Florida, Louisiana, Alabama, and Mississippi, forbidding to negroes the use of firearms: in two of these states absolutely, in one except by license, and in the other of such arms only as were "appropriate for purposes of war." Recollections of the negro insurrection headed by Nat Turner, coupled with predictions long ago made by Mr. Calhoun, and frequently by others during and preceding the Civil

War, had inspired in the South a very general fear that, in favor-
ing localities, the suddenly emancipated slaves might attempt to
repeat the massacres of San Domingo. In two of the states thus
forbidding or limiting the use of firearms the negro was in the
majority; in the other two there were "negro belts," where the
few whites would be helpless in case of an insurrection.

The most indefensible provision anywhere found by the
writer is a statute of Mississippi, enacting that, while freedmen
might hold personal property, they should not be allowed to
lease lands or tenements "except in towns or cities, where the
corporate authorities shall control the same." How much of this
enactment was the result of pure prejudice, and how much of it
came from the bogy of negro supremacy in a state in parts of
which the negro was in numbers as overwhelming as he had been
in San Domingo, the reader will determine for himself.

Much was yet to be learned about the freedman by both
Southerner and Northerner. The one was to find out how peaceful, the other how incapable as a voter, the freedman was.

There was little chance for moderation in public sentiment or
for deliberate action by Congress, when Southern people, in
constant dread, were watching and guarding against insurrection, which they even feared might be prompted by agents of
the Freedmen's Bureau; and when, at the same time, Northern
people, with their hearts full of sympathy for the helpless and
hapless freedmen, were daily watching the reports of that Bureau for stories of cruelty by the former masters. The friction,
reasonably to be expected, between the master race on the one
hand, almost all of them with the domineering blood of the
Anglo-Saxon in their veins, few of them saints and all the rest
sinners, and the negro on the other, now dazed by the blinding
light of sudden freedom, would naturally be enough, even without official intermeddling, to cause almost any one to believe or
to do anything toward which either prejudice or philanthropy
might incline him. Nevertheless, there were prominent Republi-

cans who took no stock in the continued scrutiny by the North of the relations between whites and blacks in the South. Among these was the head of Lincoln's and Johnson's Cabinet, Mr. Seward, who said in an interview in April, 1866: "The North has nothing to do with the negroes. . . . They are not of our race. They will find their place. They must take their level. The laws of political economy will determine their position, and the relations of the two races. Congress cannot contravene those."

But Mr. Seward and his views were then in a woeful minority.

Only one of the late Confederate states had legislated in relation to the negro when Congress met, December 4, 1865, and yet the members of that body had already made up their minds against Mr. Johnson's plan of reconstruction.

The first step of this Congress was the passage, by practically a solid party vote, of the celebrated "Concurrent Resolution" to inquire by a Committee of Fifteen into the condition of the late Confederate states; the next was the passage in the House, December 14, of a resolution referring to that Committee of Fifteen every question relating to conditions in the late Confederate states, and to admit no member from these states until the committee had reported; then came the defeat of the Voorhees resolution, indorsing the presidential plan. The Republicans, in the votes on all these measures, presented practically a solid front, while the Democrats were unanimous in opposition. The action of the Senate was on like lines. In the language of Mr. Stevens, Congress was already determined "to take no account of the aggregation of whitewashed rebels who, without any legal authority, have assembled in the capitals of the late rebel states and simulated legislative bodies."

Reconstruction was already a party question. Mr. Stevens, the leader of the radicals, said, during these proceedings, on the floor of the House, December 14, 1865: "According to my judgment, they [the insurrectionary states] ought never to be recognized as capable of acting in the Union, or of being recognized as valid states, until the Constitution shall have been so amended as to make it what its makers intended, *and so as to secure perpetual ascendency to the party of the Union.*"

A sample of the arguments for the Concurrent Resolution is the following, by a prominent member, Mr. Shellabarger, in answer to Mr. Raymond: "They framed iniquity and universal murder into law. . . . Their pirates burned your unarmed commerce upon every sea. They carved the bones of your dead heroes into ornaments, and drank from goblets made out of their skulls. They poisoned your fountains, put mines under your soldiers' prisons, organized bands whose leaders were concealed in your homes; and commissions ordered the torch and yellow fever to be carried to your citizens and to your women and children. They planned one universal bonfire of the North from Lake Ontario to the Missouri," etc.

Moderation was out of the question. A few conservative Republicans, who, like Mr. Raymond, of New York, stood out for Mr. Johnson's policy, were trampled under the feet of the majority. Others, though halting now and then, kept in line with the party which was steadily marching forward to the view that was already held by the radicals, and afterward expressed by Mr. Sumner in debate upon the bill for suffrage in the District of Columbia: "Nothing is clearer than the absolute necessity for suffrage for all colored persons in the disorganized states. It will not be enough if you give it to those who read and write; you will not in this way acquire the voting force which you need there for the protection of Unionists, whether black or white. You will not secure the new allies who are essential to the national cause."

To reach this goal there were many obstacles to be overcome, and time was necessary. The plan of the radicals included legislation relating to freedmen; there was good reason to expect hostility from the Supreme Court, and Southerners did not foresee how a square decision from that tribunal could be avoided;

it included constitutional amendments; three fourths of the states only could amend the Constitution, and several of the Northern states were hostile to negro suffrage; while, if the policy entered upon should fail, the failure would be disastrous. The Democrats in Congress had allied themselves with the cause of the Southern whites, and, as Mr. Stevens expressed it on the floor of the House, if negroes were not to have the ballot, the representatives from the Southern states, with the Democrats "that would be elected in the best of times at the North," would control the country.

The radicals were looking hopefully to the investigation of the Committee of Fifteen, under the Concurrent Resolution, of which Mr. Seward said (Bancroft's Seward, p. 454) it "was not a plan for reconstruction, but a plan for indefinite delay." The committee was composed of twelve Republicans and three Democrats, and of them Mr. Blaine says (Twenty Years in Congress, vol. ii. p. 127): "It was forseen that in an especial degree the fortunes of the Republican party would be in the keeping of the fifteen men who might be chosen." This committee was appointed in December, 1865, continued its investigations until June, 1866, when, dividing on strictly party lines, the majority made its report June 18, and the minority June 22.

The majority report discussed at length theories of reconstruction, and bitterly condemned the plan of the President. As to conditions in the South, it found that the Freedmen's Bureau was "almost universally hated," and that "the feeling in many portions towards the emancipated slaves, especially among the uneducated and ignorant, is one of vindictive and malicious hatred. This deep-seated prejudice against color is assiduously cultivated by the public journals, and leads to acts of cruelty, oppression, and murder, which the local authorities are at no pains to prevent or punish."

The committee went on to recommend that Congress should not admit the late Confederate states to representation "without first providing such constitutional or other guaranties as will

tend to secure the civil rights of all the citizens of the Republic,"
the disfranchisement of a portion, etc. As to the nature of the
guaranties to be required there was in this report nothing definite. The three minority members, in their report, vigorously
combated the views of the majority.

Mr. Stevens had reported, January 31, 1866, and the House
had passed, a proposition for a constitutional amendment providing that, whenever suffrage was denied on account of race or
color, the persons so denied suffrage should be excluded from
the basis of representation. But there was no promise that such
amendment, if adopted, should be taken as a settlement. The
amendment, however, was never to be submitted to the states, as
Mr. Sumner and other radicals joined with the Democrats and
conservative Republicans, and defeated it in the Senate.

Both Democrats and Republicans were now treating all measures affecting the South as political, and the late Confederate
states were being counted as in the Union for the purpose of
passing on constitutional amendments, while their governments
were held as "revolutionary, null, and void" for all other purposes. Nothing could more conclusively illustrate the intense
partisanship of the hour.

The fairest chance the Southern state governments, as set up
by Johnson, had to stem the tide that was setting in against them
—but it is doubtful whether that could have succeeded—was by
unanimously ratifying the Fourteenth Amendment. Had this
amendment been accepted by both sides as a settlement, it would
have reduced the representation of the late slave states and left
them in control of suffrage. But this article disfranchised all
Southerners of prominence and experience, and Southern people
could not bring themselves to vote for the degradation of those
whom they had honored and trusted. Johnson, too, now their
friend and political leader, advised against it; so did Northern
Democrats. It was a political fight to a finish between the prostrate ex-Confederates, without representation in Congress and

without an acknowledged vote anywhere, aided by the President, a handful of Democrats in Congress, and an unknown number of sympathizers in the North, on the one side, and the Republican party in unmistakable control of Congress on the other. The bill for the extension of the Freedmen's Bureau, which failed to pass over Johnson's veto, and the civil rights bill, which did pass over a veto—these, and the angry discussions over them in the spring of 1866, only intensified, North and South, the bitterness of the struggle in progress.

If Mr. Lincoln had lived, and had carried on, as the speech in answer to a serenade just before his death indicates he would have done, the policy embodied in the North Carolina proclamation, approved by him shortly before his death,[1] and used by his successor as the basis of his policy, he would have had before him the same open field and the same nine months preceding the meeting of Congress that were before Johnson; and though it would have been a strange spectacle to see the great Republican chieftain politically allied with ex-Confederates, one cannot avoid the conclusion that, tactful and at the same time great-hearted as he was, he would have been continually pointing out to Southerners the breakers that they did not, and he did, see ahead. His influence, too, with his own party, after the successful termination of the war, would have given him a measure of control over his party that Johnson did not possess.

Mr. Johnson was much abused for having "deserted" the party that had honored him, and now that the fight was on, instead of the coolness and skill of a gladiator, he manifested only the qualities of an angry bull rushing at a red rag. In a public speech, al-

---

[1] "The very same instrument for restoring the national authority over North Carolina, and placing her where she stood before her attempted secession, which had been approved by Mr. Lincoln, was by Mr. Stanton presented at the first Cabinet meeting which was held at the Executive Mansion after Mr. Lincoln's death, and having been carefully considered at two or three meetings, was adopted as the reconstruction policy of the [Johnson's] Administration." (McCulloch's *Men and Measures*, p. 378.)

luding to some charge that he had played Judas, he said: "If I have played the Judas, who has been my Christ that I have played the Judas with? Was it Thad Stevens? Was it Wendell Phillips? Was it Charles Sumner?"

Numerous conventions, state and national, were now, in 1866, being held, all devoted to the manufacture of public opinion for and against the Johnson plan of reconstruction.

No two eras in our history differ more widely than the epoch-making years 1787 and 1866. In the one, statesmen were sitting with closed doors to formulate, uninfluenced by outside discussion, the Constitution which is the most perfect work of man. In the other, with doors wide open, members of both political parties uttering fiery declarations which were echoed and re-ëchoed all over the land, the two houses of Congress as political bodies, with passion at white heat, shaped the policy according to which the chief corner stone of the old Constitution—the suffrage on which it rested—was to be remodeled; and the trend of all the work of the session of 1865–66 was in the direction of the guaranties demanded by Mr. Stevens and Mr. Sumner.

That policy, when the session had closed, was submitted to the Northern voters in the congressional elections of 1866. It was overwhelmingly approved; and at the last session of that Congress the act of March 2, 1867, was passed, reconstructing the states on the basis of universal negro suffrage, to which the Fifteenth Amendment, intended to secure the rights thus granted, was but a corollary—both, as we have seen, begotten of partisanship out of philanthropy; and this was not the first, nor has it been the last, of these *liaisons*.

It is not making any new or startling assertion to say that negro suffrage was a failure. It did not give Republican control at the South, except for a brief period, and it did not benefit, but injured, the freedman; it made unavoidable in the South the color line, and *impossible there two capable political parties, of which all men North and South alike, now see the crying need.*

The negro had, when suddenly emancipated, one recourse: he was by training a good laborer. The pathway was wide open before him to profit by experience based upon the results of continued industry. Laws like those we have noted, repressing idleness, even though unnecessarily severe, as some of them undoubtedly were, would have given him a continuing forward impulse in what was his only possible line of betterment; for the lesson of self-support is a prerequisite of all development. In Mr. Seward's language, the negro would have found his place.

To import the ex-slave into politics was to make a parasite of a plant that needed to strike its roots deep into the earth. To implant within him the thought that he might live without work was an egregious error. Influential negroes, those who should have led in industry and thrift, not only themselves deserted the cotton field for the field of politics, but drew others after them to march in processions and listen to discussions no syllable of which was comprehensible save only appeals to race antagonism. The consequences of the mistake then made have come down to this day; and as to some of them, at least, whites and blacks are now working together for relief.

Professor W. H. Council, the able negro president of the college at Huntsville, Alabama, voiced the present best Southern thought when he said, in his annual address to his colored students, in October last: "As our footsteps diverge from political walks, they approach industrial success and true citizenship. The negro will grow strong and grow into usefulness in proportion to his contribution to industrial development, and not political strife."

The Freedmen's Bureau

W. E. BURGHARDT
DU BOIS

The problem of the twentieth century is the problem of the color line; the relation of the darker to the lighter races of men in Asia and Africa, in America and the islands of the sea. It was a phase of this problem that caused the Civil War; and however much they who marched south and north in 1861 may have fixed on the technical points of union and local autonomy as a shibboleth, all nevertheless knew, as we know, that the question of Negro slavery was the deeper cause of the conflict. Curious it was, too, how this deeper question ever forced itself to the surface, despite effort and disclaimer. No sooner had Northern armies touched Southern soil than this old question, newly guised, sprang from the earth—What shall be done with slaves? Peremptory military commands, this way and that, could not answer the query; the Emancipation Proclamation seemed but to broaden and intensify the difficulties; and so at last there arose in the South a government of men called the Freedmen's Bureau, which lasted, legally, from 1865 to 1872, but in a sense from 1861 to 1876, and which sought to settle the Negro problems in the United States of America.

It is the aim of this essay to study the Freedmen's Bureau—the occasion of its rise, the character of its work, and its final success and failure—not only as a part of American history, but above all as one of the most singular and interesting of the attempts made by a great nation to grapple with vast problems of race and social conditon.

No sooner had the armies, east and west, penetrated Virginia and Tennessee than fugitive slaves appeared within their lines. They came at night, when the flickering camp fires of the blue hosts shone like vast unsteady stars along the black horizon: old men, and thin, with gray and tufted hair; women with frightened eyes, dragging whimpering, hungry children; men and girls, stalwart and gaunt—a horde of starving vagabonds, homeless, helpless, and pitiable in their dark distress. Two methods of treating these newcomers seemed equally logical to opposite sorts of minds. Said some, "We have nothing to do with slaves." "Hereafter," commanded Halleck, "no slaves should be allowed to come into your lines at all; if any come without your knowledge, when owners call for them, deliver them." But others said, "We take grain and fowl; why not slaves?" Whereupon Fremont, as early as August, 1861, declared the slaves of Missouri rebels free. Such radical action was quickly countermanded, but at the same time the opposite policy could not be enforced; some of the black refugees declared themselves freemen, others showed their masters had deserted them, and still others were captured with forts and plantations. Evidently, too, slaves were a source of strength to the Confederacy, and were being used as laborers and producers. "They constitute a military resource," wrote the Secretary of War, late in 1861; "and being such, that they should not be turned over to the enemy is too plain to discuss." So the tone of the army chiefs changed, Congress forbade the rendition of fugitives, and Butler's "contrabands" were welcomed as military laborers. This complicated rather than solved the problem; for now the scattering fugitives became a steady stream, which flowed faster as the armies marched.

Then the long-headed man, with care-chiseled face, who sat in the White House, saw the inevitable, and emancipated the slaves of rebels on New Year's, 1863. A month later Congress called earnestly for the Negro soldiers whom the act of July, 1862, had half grudgingly allowed to enlist. Thus the barriers were leveled, and the deed was done. The stream of fugitives swelled to a flood, and anxious officers kept inquiring: "What must be done with slaves arriving almost daily? Am I to find food and shelter for women and children?"

It was a Pierce of Boston who pointed out the way, and thus became in a sense the founder of the Freedmen's Bureau. Being specially detailed from the ranks to care for the freedmen at Fortress Monroe, he afterward founded the celebrated Port Royal experiment and started the Freedmen's Aid Societies. Thus, under the timid Treasury officials and bold army officers, Pierce's plan widened and developed. At first, the able-bodied men were enlisted as soldiers or hired as laborers, the women and children were herded into central camps under guard, and "superintendents of contrabands" multiplied here and there. Centres of massed freedmen arose at Fortress Monroe, Va., Washington, D. C., Beaufort and Port Royal, S. C., New Orleans, La., Vicksburg and Corinth, Miss., Columbus, Ky., Cairo, Ill., and elsewhere, and the army chaplains found here new and fruitful fields.

Then came the Freedmen's Aid Societies, born of the touching appeals for relief and help from these centres of distress. There was the American Missionary Association, sprung from the *Amistad,* and now full grown for work, the various church organizations, the National Freedmen's Relief Association, the American Freedmen's Union, the Western Freedmen's Aid

Commission—in all fifty or more active organizations, which sent clothes, money, schoolbooks, and teachers southward. All they did was needed, for the destitution of the freedmen was often reported as "too appalling for belief," and the situation was growing daily worse rather than better.

And daily, too, it seemed more plain that this was no ordinary matter of temporary relief, but a national crisis; for here loomed a labor problem of vast dimensions. Masses of Negroes stood idle, or, if they worked spasmodically, were never sure of pay; and if perchance they received pay, squandered the new thing thoughtlessly. In these and in other ways were camp life and the new liberty demoralizing the freedmen. The broader economic organization thus clearly demanded sprang up here and there as accident and local conditions determined. Here again Pierce's Port Royal plan of leased plantations and guided workmen pointed out the rough way. In Washington, the military governor, at the urgent appeal of the superintendent, opened confiscated estates to the cultivation of the fugitives, and there in the shadow of the dome gathered black farm villages. General Dix gave over estates to the freedmen of Fortress Monroe, and so on through the South. The government and the benevolent societies furnished the means of cultivation, and the Negro turned again slowly to work. The systems of control, thus started, rapidly grew, here and there, into strange little governments, like that of General Banks in Louisiana, with its 90,000 black subjects, its 50,000 guided laborers, and its annual budget of $100,000 and more. It made out 4000 pay rolls, registered all freedmen, inquired into grievances and redressed them, laid and collected taxes, and established a system of public schools. So too Colonel Eaton, the superintendent of Tennessee and Arkansas, ruled over 100,000, leased and cultivated 7000 acres of cotton land, and furnished food for 10,000 paupers. In South Carolina was General Saxton, with his deep interest in black folk. He succeeded Pierce and the Treasury officials, and sold forfeited estates, leased abandoned plantations, encouraged schools, and received from Sherman, after the terribly picturesque march to the sea, thousands of the wretched camp followers.

Three characteristic things one might have seen in Sherman's raid through Georgia, which threw the new situation in deep and shadowy relief: the Conqueror, the Conquered, and the Negro. Some see all significance in the grim front of the destroyer, and some in the bitter sufferers of the lost cause. But to me neither soldier nor fugitive speaks with so deep a meaning as that dark and human cloud that clung like remorse on the rear of those swift columns, swelling at times to half their size, almost engulfing and choking them. In vain were they ordered back, in vain were bridges hewn from beneath their feet; on they trudged and writhed and surged, until they rolled into Savannah, a starved and naked horde of tens of thousands. There too came the characteristic military remedy: "The islands from Charleston south, the abandoned ricefields along the rivers for thirty miles back from the sea, and the country bordering the St. John's River, Florida, are reserved and set apart for the settlement of Negroes now made free by act of war." So read the celebrated field order.

All these experiments, orders, and systems were bound to attract and perplex the government and the nation. Directly after the Emancipation Proclamation, Representative Eliot had introduced a bill creating a Bureau of Emancipation, but it was never reported. The following June, a committee of inquiry, appointed by the Secretary of War, reported in favor of a temporary bureau for the "improvement, protection, and employment of refugee freedmen," on much the same lines as were afterward followed. Petitions came in to President Lincoln from distinguished citizens and organizations, strongly urging a comprehensive and unified plan of dealing with the freedmen, under a bureau which should be "charged with the study of plans and execution of measures for easily guiding, and in every way judiciously and humanely aiding, the passage of our emancipated and yet to be emancipated blacks from the old condition of forced labor to their new state of voluntary industry."

Some half-hearted steps were early taken by the government to put both freedmen and abandoned estates under the supervision of the Treasury officials. Laws of 1863 and 1864 directed them to take charge of and lease abandoned lands for periods not exceeding twelve months, and to "provide in such leases or otherwise for the employment and general welfare" of the freedmen. Most of the army officers looked upon this as a welcome relief from perplexing "Negro affairs"; but the Treasury hesitated and blundered, and although it leased large quantities of land and employed many Negroes, especially along the Mississippi, yet it left the virtual control of the laborers and their relations to their neighbors in the hands of the army.

In March, 1864, Congress at last turned its attention to the subject, and the House passed a bill, by a majority of two, establishing a Bureau for Freedmen in the War Department. Senator Sumner, who had charge of the bill in the Senate, argued that freedmen and abandoned lands ought to be under the same department, and reported a substitute for the House bill, attaching the Bureau to the Treasury Department. This bill passed, but too late for action in the House. The debates wandered over the whole policy of the administration and the general question of slavery, without touching very closely the specific merits of the measure in hand.

Meantime the election took place, and the administration, returning from the country with a vote of renewed confidence, addressed itself to the matter more seriously. A confidence between the houses agreed upon a carefully drawn measure which contained the chief provisions of Charles Sumner's bill, but made the proposed organization a department independent of both the War and Treasury officials. The bill was conservative, giving the new department "general superintendence of all freedmen." It was to "establish regulations" for them, protect them, lease them lands, adjust their wages, and appear in civil and military courts as their "next friend." There were many limitations attached to the powers thus granted, and the organization was made permanent. Nevertheless, the Senate defeated the bill, and a new conference committee was appointed. This committee reported a new bill, February 28, which was whirled through just as the session closed, and which became the act of 1865 establishing in the War Department a "Bureau of Refugees, Freedmen, and Abandoned Lands."

This last compromise was a hasty bit of legislation, vague and uncertain in outline. A Bureau was created, "to continue during the present War of Rebellion, and for one year thereafter," to which was given "the supervision and management of all abandoned lands, and the control of all subjects relating to refugees and freedmen," under "such rules and regulations as may be presented by the head of the Bureau and approved by the President." A commissioner, appointed by the President and Senate, was to control the Bureau, with an office force not exceeding ten clerks. The President might also appoint assistant commissioners in the seceded states, and to all these offices military officials might be detailed at regular pay. The Secretary of War could issue rations, clothing, and fuel to the destitute, and all abandoned property was placed in the hands of the Bureau for eventual lease and sale to ex-slaves in forty-acre parcels.

Thus did the United States government definitely assume charge of the emancipated Negro as the ward of the nation. It was a tremendous undertaking. Here, at a stroke of the pen, was erected a government of millions of men—and not ordinary men, either, but black men emasculated by a peculiarly complete system of slavery, centuries old; and now, suddenly, violently, they come into a new birthright, at a time of war and passion, in the midst of the stricken, embittered population of their former masters. Any man might well have hesitated to assume charge of such a work, with vast responsibilities, indefinite powers, and limited resources. Probably no one but a soldier would have answered such a call promptly; and indeed no one but a soldier could be called, for Congress had appropriated no money for salaries and expenses.

Less than a month after the weary emancipator passed to his rest, his successor assigned Major General Oliver O. Howard to duty as commissioner of the new Bureau. He was a Maine man, then only thirty-five years of age. He had marched with Sherman to the sea, had fought well at Gettysburg, and had but a year before been assigned to the command of the Department of Tennessee. An honest and sincere man, with rather too much faith in human nature, little aptitude for systematic business and intricate detail, he was nevertheless conservative, hard-working, and, above all, acquainted at first-hand with much of the work before him. And of that work it has been truly said, "No approximately correct history of civilization can ever be written which does not throw out in bold relief, as one of the great landmarks of political and social progress, the organization and administration of the Freedmen's Bureau."

On May 12, 1865, Howard was appointed, and he assumed the duties of his office promptly on the 15th, and began examining the field of work. A curious mess he looked upon: little despotisms, communistic experiments, slavery, peonage, business speculations, organized charity, unorganized almsgiving—all reeling on under the guise of helping the freedman, and all enshrined in the smoke and blood of war and the cursing and silence of angry men. On May 19 the new government—for a government it really was—issued its constitution; commissioners were to be appointed in each of the seceded states, who were to take charge of "all subjects relating to refugees and freedmen," and all relief and rations were to be given by their consent alone. The Bureau invited continued coöperation with benevolent societies, and declared, "It will be the object of all commissioners to introduce practicable systems of compensated labor," and to establish schools. Forthwith nine assistant commissioners were appointed. They were to hasten to their fields of work; seek gradually to close relief establishments, and make the destitute self-supporting; act as courts of law where there were no courts, or where Negroes were not recognized in them as free; establish the institution of marriage among ex-slaves, and keep records; see that freedmen were free to choose their employers, and help in making fair contracts for them; and finally, the circular said, "Simple good faith, for which we hope on all hands for those concerned in the passing away of slavery, will especially relieve the assistant commissioners in the discharge of their duties toward the freedmen, as well as promote the general welfare."

No sooner was the work thus started, and the general system and local organization in some measure begun, than two grave difficulties appeared which changed largely the theory and outcome of Bureau work. First, there were the abandoned lands of the South. It had long been the more or less definitely expressed theory of the North that all the chief problems of emancipation might be settled by establishing the slaves on the forfeited lands of their masters—a sort of poetic justice, said some. But this poetry done into solemn prose meant either wholesale confiscation of private property in the South, or vast appropriations. Now Congress had not appropriated a cent, and no sooner did the proclamations of general amnesty appear than the 800,000 acres of abandoned lands in the hands of the Freedmen's Bureau melted quickly away. The second difficulty lay in perfecting the local organization of the Bureau throughout the wide field of work. Making a new machine and sending out officials of duly ascertained fitness for a great work of social reform is no child's task; but this task was even harder, for a new central organization had to be fitted on a heterogeneous and confused but already existing system of relief and control of ex-slaves; and the agents available for this work must be sought for in an army still busy with war operations— men in the very nature of the case ill fitted for delicate social work—or among the questionable camp followers of an invading host. Thus, after a year's work, vigorously as it was pushed, the problem looked even more difficult to grasp and solve than at the beginning. Nevertheless, three things that year's work did, well worth the doing: it relieved a vast amount of physical suffering; it transported 7,000 fugitives from congested centres back to the farm; and, best of all, it inaugurated the crusade of the New England schoolma'am.

The annals of this Ninth Crusade are yet to be written, the tale of a mission that seemed to our age far more quixotic than the quest of St. Louis seemed to his. Behind the mists of ruin and rapine waved the calico dresses of women who dared, and after the hoarse mouthings of the field guns rang the rhythm of the alphabet. Rich and poor they were, serious and curious. Bereaved now of a father, now of a brother, now of more than these, they came seeking a life work in planting New England schoolhouses among the white and black of the South. They did their work well. In that first year they taught 100,000 souls, and more.

Evidently, Congress must soon legislate again on the hastily organized Bureau, which had so quickly grown into wide significance and vast possibilities. An institution such as that was well-nigh as difficult to end as to begin. Early in 1866 Congress took up the matter, when Senator Trumbull, of Illinois, introduced a bill to extend the Bureau and enlarge its powers. This measure received, at the hands of Congress, far more thorough discussion and attention than its predecessor. The war cloud had thinned enough to allow a clearer conception of the work of emancipation. The champions of the bill argued that the strenthening of the Freedmen's Bureau was still a military necessity; that it was needed for the proper carrying out of the Thirteenth Amendment, and was a work of sheer justice to the exslave, at a trifling cost to the government. The opponents of the measure declared that the war was over, and the necessity for war measures past; that the Bureau, by reason of its extraordinary powers, was clearly unconstitutional in time of peace, and was destined to irritate the South and pauperize the freedmen, at final cost of possibly hundreds of millions. Two of these arguments were unanswered, and indeed unanswerable: the one that the extraordinary powers of the Bureau threatened the civil rights of all citizens; and the other that the government must have power to do what manifestly must be done, and that present abandonment of the freedmen meant their practical reenslavement. The bill which finally passed enlarged and made permanent the Freedmen's Bureau. It was promptly vetoed by President Johnson, as "unconstitutional," "unnecessary," and "extrajudicial," and failed of passage over the veto. Meantime, however, the breach between Congress and the President began to broaden, and a modified form of the lost bill was finally passed over the President's second veto, July 16.

The act of 1866 gave the Freedmen's Bureau its final form— the form by which it will be known to posterity and judged of men. It extended the existence of the Bureau to July, 1868; it authorized additional assistant commissioners, the retention of army officers mustered out of regular service, the sale of certain forfeited lands to freedmen on nominal terms, the sale of Confederate public property for Negro schools, and a wider field of judicial interpretation and cognizance. The government of the unreconstructed South was thus put very largely in the hands of the Freedmen's Bureau, especially as in many cases the departmental military commander was now made also assistant commissioner. It was thus that the Freedmen's Bureau became a full-fledged government of men. It made laws, executed them and interpreted them; it laid and collected taxes, defined and punished crime, maintained and used military force, and dictated such measures as it thought necessary and proper for the accomplishment of its varied ends. Naturally, all these powers are not exercised continuously nor to their fullest extent; and yet, as

General Howard has said, "scarcely any subject that has to be legislated upon in civil society failed, at one time or another, to demand the action of this singular Bureau."

To understand and criticise intelligently so vast a work, one must not forget an instant the drift of things in the later sixties: Lee had surrendered, Lincoln was dead, and Johnson and Congress were at loggerheads; the Thirteenth Amendment was adopted, the Fourteenth pending, and the Fifteenth declared in force in 1870. Guerrilla raiding, the ever present flickering afterflame of war, was spending its force against the Negroes, and all the Southern land was awakening as from some wild dream to poverty and social revolution. In a time of perfect calm, amid willing neighbors and streaming wealth, the social uplifting of 4,000,000 slaves to an assured and self-sustaining place in the body politic and economic would have been an herculean task; but when to the inherent difficulties of so delicate and nice a social operation were added the spite and hate of conflict, the Hell of War; when suspicion and cruelty were rife, and gaunt Hunger wept beside Bereavement—in such a case, the work of any instrument of social regeneration was in large part foredoomed to failure. The very name of the Bureau stood for a thing in the South which for two centuries and better men had refused even to argue—that life amid free Negroes was simply unthinkable, the maddest of experiments. The agents which the Bureau could command varied all the way from unselfish philanthropists to narrow-minded busybodies and thieves; and even though it be true that the average was far better than the worst, it was the one fly that helped to spoil the ointment. Then, amid all this crouched the freed slave, bewildered between friend and foe. He had emerged from slavery: not the worst slavery in the world, not a slavery that made all life unbearable—rather, a slavery that had here and there much of kindness, fidelity, and happiness—but withal slavery, which, so far as human aspiration and desert were concerned, classed the black man and the ox together. And the Negro knew full well that, whatever their deeper convictions may have been, Southern men had fought with desperate energy to perpetuate this slavery, under which the black masses, with half-articulate thought, had writhed and shivered. They welcomed freedom with a cry. They fled to the friends that had freed them. They shrank from the master who still strove for their chains. So the cleft between the white and black South grew. Idle to say it never should have been; it was as inevitable as its results were pitiable. Curiously incongruous elements were left arrayed against each other: the North, the government, the carpetbagger, and the slave, here; and there, all the South that was white, whether gentleman or vagabond, honest man or rascal, lawless murderer or martyr to duty.

Thus it is doubly difficult to write of this period calmly, so intense was the feeling, so mighty the human passions, that swayed and blinded men. Amid it all two figures ever stand to typify that day to coming men: the one a gray-haired gentleman, whose fathers had quit themselves like men, whose sons lay in nameless graves; who bowed to the evil of slavery because its abolition boded untold ill to all; who stood at last, in the evening of life, a blighted, ruined form, with hate in his eyes. And the other, a form hovering dark and mother-like, her awful face black with the mists of centuries, had aforetime bent in love over her white master's cradle, rocked his sons and daughters to sleep, and closed in death the sunken eyes of his wife to the world; ay, too, had laid herself low to his lust and borne a tawny man child to the world, only to see her dark boy's limbs scattered to the winds by midnight marauders riding after Damned Niggers. These were the saddest sights of that woeful day; and no man clasped the hands of these two passing figures of the present-past; but hating they went to their long home, and hating their children's children live to-day.

Here, then, was the field of work for the Freedmen's Bureau; and since, with some hesitation, it was continued by the act of

1868 till 1869, let us look upon four years of its work as a whole. There were, in 1868, 900 Bureau officials scattered from Washington to Texas, ruling, directly and indirectly, many millions of men. And the deeds of these rulers fall mainly under seven heads —the relief of physical suffering, the overseeing of the beginnings of free labor, the buying and selling of land, the establishment of schools, the paying of bounties, the administration of justice, and the financiering of all these activities. Up to June, 1869, over half a million patients had been treated by Bureau physicians and surgeons, and sixty hospitals and asylums had been in operation. In fifty months of work 21,000,000 free rations were distributed at a cost of over $4,000,000—beginning at the rate of 30,000 rations a day in 1865, and discontinuing in 1869. Next came the difficult question of labor. First, 30,000 black men were transported from the refuges and relief stations back to the farms, back to the critical trial of a new way of working. Plain, simple instructions went out from Washington, —the freedom of laborers to choose employers, no fixed rates of wages, no peonage or forced labor. So far so good; but where local agents differed *toto cælo* in capacity and character, where the personnel was continually changing, the outcome was varied. The largest element of success lay in the fact that the majority of the freedmen were willing, often eager, to work. So contracts were written—50,000 in a single state—laborers advised, wages guaranteed, and employers supplied. In truth, the organization became a vast labor bureau; not perfect, indeed— notably defective here and there—but on the whole, considering the situation, successful beyond the dreams of thoughtful men. The two great obstacles which confronted the officers at every turn were the tyrant and the idler: the slaveholder, who believed slavery was right, and was determined to perpetuate it under another name; and the freedman, who regarded freedom as perpetual rest. These were the Devil and the Deep Sea.

In the work of establishing the Negroes as peasant proprietors the Bureau was severely handicapped, as I have shown. Nevertheless, something was done. Abandoned lands were leased so long as they remained in the hands of the Bureau, and a total revenue of $400,000 derived from black tenants. Some other lands to which the nation had gained title were sold, and public lands were opened for the settlement of the few blacks who had tools and capital. The vision of landowning, however, the righteous and reasonable ambition for forty acres and a mule which filled the freedmen's dreams, was doomed in most cases to disappointment. And those men of marvelous hind-sight, who today are seeking to preach the Negro back to the soil, know well, or ought to know, that it was here, in 1865, that the finest opportunity of binding the black peasant to the soil was lost. Yet, with help and striving, the Negro gained some land, and by 1874, in the one state of Georgia, owned near 350,000 acres.

The greatest success of the Freedmen's Bureau lay in the planting of the free school among Negroes, and the idea of free elementary education among all classes in the South. It not only called the schoolmistress through the benevolent agencies, and built them schoolhouses, but it helped discover and support such apostles of human development as Edmund Ware, Erastus Cravath, and Samuel Armstrong. State superintendents of education were appointed, and by 1870 150,000 children were in school. The opposition to Negro education was bitter in the South, for the South believed an educated Negro to be a dangerous Negro. And the South was not wholly wrong; for education among all kinds of men always has had, and always will have, an element of danger and revolution, of dissatisfaction and discontent. Nevertheless, men strive to know. It was some inkling of this paradox, even in the unquiet days of the Bureau, that allayed an opposition to human training, which still to-day lies smouldering, but not flaming. Fisk, Atlanta, Howard, and Hampton were founded in these days, and nearly $6,000,000 was expended in five years for educational work, $750,000 of which came from the freedmen themselves.

Such contributions, together with the buying of land and various other enterprises, showed that the ex-slave was handling some free capital already. The chief initial source of this was labor in the army, and his pay and bounty as a soldier. Payments to Negro soldiers were at first complicated by the ignorance of the recipients, and the fact that the quotas of colored regiments from Northern states were largely filled by recruits from the South, unknown to their fellow soldiers. Consequently, payments were accompanied by such frauds that Congress, by joint resolution in 1867, put the whole matter in the hands of the Freedmen's Bureau. In two years $6,000,000 was thus distributed to 5000 claimants, and in the end the sum exceeded $8,000,000. Even in this system fraud was frequent; but still the work put needed capital in the hands of practical paupers, and some, at least, was well spent.

The most perplexing and least successful part of the Bureau's work lay in the exercise of its judicial functions. In a distracted land where slavery had hardly fallen, to keep the strong from wanton abuse of the weak, and the weak from gloating insolently over the half-shorn strength of the strong, was a thankless, hopeless task. The former masters of the land were peremptorily ordered about, seized and imprisoned, and punished over and again, with scant courtesy from army officers. The former slaves were intimidated, beaten, raped, and butchered by angry and revengeful men. Bureau courts tended to become centres simply for punishing whites, while the regular civil courts tended to become solely institutions for perpetuating the slavery of blacks. Almost every law and method ingenuity could devise was employed by the legislatures to reduce the Negroes to serfdom—to make them the slaves of the state, if not of individual owners; while the Bureau officials too often were found striving to put the "bottom rail on top," and give the freedmen a power and independence which they could not yet use. It is all well enough for us of another generation to wax wise with advice to those who bore the burden in the heat of the day. It is full easy now to see that the man who lost home, fortune, and family at a stroke, and saw his land ruled by "mules and niggers," was really benefited by the passing of slavery. It is not difficult now to say to the young freedman, cheated and cuffed about, who has seen his father's head beaten to a jelly and his own mother namelessly assaulted, that the meek shall inherit the earth. Above all, nothing is more convenient than to heap on the Freedmen's Bureau all the evils of that evil day, and damn it utterly for every mistake and blunder that was made.

All this is easy, but it is neither sensible nor just. Some one had blundered, but that was long before Oliver Howard was born; there was criminal aggression and heedless neglect, but without some system of control there would have been far more than there was. Had that control been from within, the Negro would have been reënslaved, to all intents and purposes. Coming as the control did from without, perfect men and methods would have bettered all things; and even with imperfect agents and questionable methods, the work accomplished was not undeserving of much commendation. The regular Bureau court consisted of one representative of the employer, one of the Negro, and one of the Bureau. If the Bureau could have maintained a perfectly judicial attitude, this arrangement would have been ideal, and must in time have gained confidence; but the nature of its other activities and the character of its personnel prejudiced the Bureau in favor of the black litigants, and led without doubt to much injustice and annoyance. On the other hand, to leave the Negro in the hands of Southern courts was impossible.

What the Freedmen's Bureau cost the nation is difficult to determine accurately. Its methods of bookkeeping were not good, and the whole system of its work and records partook of the hurry and turmoil of the time. General Howard himself disbursed some $15,000,000 during his incumbency; but this includes the bounties paid colored soldiers, which perhaps should not be counted as an expense of the Bureau. In bounties, prize money, and all other expenses, the Bureau disbursed over $20,000,000 before all of its departments were finally closed. To this ought to be added the large expenses of the various departments of Negro affairs before 1865; but these are hardly extricable from war expenditures, nor can we estimate with any accuracy the contributions of benevolent societies during all these years.

Such was the work of the Freedmen's Bureau. To sum it up in brief, we may say: it set going a system of free labor; it established the black peasant proprietor; it secured the recognition of black freemen before courts of law; it founded the free public school in the South. On the other hand, it failed to establish good will between ex-masters and freedmen; to guard its work wholly from paternalistic methods that discouraged self-reliance; to make Negroes landholders in any considerable numbers. Its successes were the result of hard work, supplemented by the aid of philanthropists and the eager striving of black men. Its failures were the result of bad local agents, inherent difficulties of the work, and national neglect. The Freedmen's Bureau expired by limitation in 1869, save its educational and bounty departments. The educational work came to an end in 1872, and General Howard's connection with the Bureau ceased at that time. The work of paying bounties was transferred to the adjutant general's office, where it was continued three or four years longer.

Such an institution, from its wide powers, great responsibilities, large control of moneys, and generally conspicuous position, was naturally open to repeated and bitter attacks. It sustained a searching congressional investigation at the instance of Fernando Wood in 1870. It was, with blunt discourtesy, transferred from Howard's control, in his absence, to the supervision of Secretary of War Belknap in 1872, on the Secretary's recommendation. Finally, in consequence of grave intimations of wrongdoing made by the Secretary and his subordinates, General Howard was court-martialed in 1874. In each of these trials, and in other attacks, the commissioner of the Freedmen's Bureau was exonerated from any willful misdoing, and his work heartily commended. Nevertheless, many unpleasant things were brought to light: the methods of transacting the business of the Bureau were faulty; several cases of defalcation among officials in the field were proven, and further frauds hinted at; there were some business transactions which savored of dangerous speculation, if not dishonesty; and, above all, the smirch of the Freedmen's Bank, which, while legally distinct from, was morally and practically a part of the Bureau, will ever blacken the record of this great institution. Not even ten additional years of slavery could have done as much to throttle the thrift of the freedmen as the mismanagement and bankruptcy of the savings bank chartered by the nation for their especial aid. Yet it is but fair to say that the perfect honesty of purpose and unselfish devotion of General Howard have passed untarnished through the fire of criticism. Not so with all his subordinates, although in the case of the great majority of these there were shown bravery and devotion to duty, even though sometimes linked to narrowness and incompetency.

The most bitter attacks on the Freedmen's Bureau were aimed not so much at its conduct or policy under the law as at the necessity for any such organization at all. Such attacks came naturally from the border states and the South, and they were summed up by Senator Davis, of Kentucky, when he moved to entitle the act of 1866 a bill "to promote strife and conflict between the white and black races . . . by a grant of unconstitutional power." The argument was of tremendous strength, but its very strength was its weakness. For, argued the plain common sense of the nation, if it is unconstitutional, unpracticable, and futile for the nation to stand guardian over its helpless wards, then there is left but one alternative: to make those wards their own guardians by arming them with the ballot. The alternative offered the nation then was not between full and restricted Negro suffrage; else every sensible man, black and white, would easily have chosen the latter. It was rather a choice between suffrage and slavery, after endless blood and gold had flowed to sweep human bondage away. Not a single Southern legislature stood ready to admit a Negro, under any conditions, to the polls; not a single Southern legislature believed free Negro labor was possible without a system of restrictions that took all its freedom away; there was scarcely a white man in the South who did not honestly regard emancipation as a crime, and its practical nullification as a duty. In such a situation, the granting of the ballot to the black man was a necessity, the very least a guilty nation could grant a wronged race. Had the opposition to government guardianship of Negroes been less bitter, and the attachment to the slave system less strong, the social seer can well imagine a far better policy: a permanent Freedmen's Bureau, with a national system of Negro schools; a carefully supervised employment and labor office; a system of impartial protection before the regular courts; and such institutions for social betterment as savings banks, land and building associations, and social settlements. All this vast expenditure of money and brains might have formed a great school of prospective citizenship, and solved in a way we have not yet solved the most perplexing and persistent of the Negro problems.

That such an institution was unthinkable in 1870 was due in part to certain acts of the Freedmen's Bureau itself. It came to regard its work as merely temporary, and Negro suffrage as a final answer to all present perplexities. The political ambition of many of its agents and protégés led it far afield into questionable activities, until the South, nursing its own deep prejudices, came easily to ignore all the good deeds of the Bureau, and hate its very name with perfect hatred. So the Freedmen's Bureau died, and its child was the Fifteenth Amendment.

The passing of a great human institution before its work is done, like the untimely passing of a single soul, but leaves a legacy of striving for other men. The legacy of the Freedmen's Bureau is the heavy heritage of this generation. Today, when new and vaster problems are destined to strain every fibre of the national mind and soul would it not be well to count this legacy honestly and carefully? For this much all men know: despite compromise, struggle, war, and struggle, the Negro is not free. In the backwoods of the Gulf states, for miles and miles, he may not leave the plantation of his birth; in well-nigh the whole rural South the black farmers are peons, bound by law and custom to an economic slavery, from which the only escape is death or the penitentiary. In the most cultured sections and cities of the South the Negroes are a segregated servile caste, with restricted rights and privileges. Before the courts, both in law and custom, they stand on a different and peculiar basis. Taxation without representation is the rule of their political life. And the result of all this is, and in nature must have been, lawlessness and crime. That is the large legacy of the Freedmen's Bureau, the work it did not do because it could not.

I have seen a land right merry with the sun; where children sing, and rolling hills lie like passioned women, wanton with harvest. And there in the King's Highway sat and sits a figure, veiled and bowed, by which the traveler's footsteps hasten as they go. On the tainted air broods fear. Three centuries' thought has been the raising and unveiling of that bowed human heart, and now, behold, my fellows, a century new for the duty and the deed. The problem of the twentieth century is the problem of the color line.

Reconstruction in South Carolina

DANIEL H. CHAMBERLAIN

The Civil War of 1861–65 (the term is used here for convenience, though it lacks perfect accuracy) was conducted in substantial or reasonable accordance with the settled rules of war; and at its close there was a large measure of liberal feeling on the part of the North toward the South, notwithstanding the murder of Mr. Lincoln. This feeling viewed the struggle as one in which both sides were sincere and patriotic (the word is used of design, but in its high and broad meaning), in which both sides were equally brave and devoted; as well as one which had come to pass quite naturally, from causes which were far deeper than politics or even than slavery. While the victorious section was enjoying the first or early sense of success, sentiments of liberality, of concord, readiness to look forward to better relations, not backward to old quarrels, statesmanlike plans or suggestions of reunion, and restoration of old associations, widely prevailed.

Two main causes now came into operation to disturb this tendency and course of feeling and events. This first of these was the existence at the North, on the part of a strenuous, ardent, vigorous minority, of a deep-seated, long-maturing, highly developed distrust of the South; a sentiment resting partly on moral antagonism to slavery, but chiefly on a feeling of dread or hatred of those who had brought on a destructive, and, worst of all, a causeless or unnecessary war. Not all of those who belonged to this class are to be described so mildly. Some, it may be said, if not many, were really moved by an unreasoning antipathy toward those whom they had so long denounced as slaveholders and rebels. Slavery abolished and rebellion subdued, their occupation was gone; and still they could not adjust themselves to a new order of things.

The other great cause of reaction from the friendly and conciliatory spirit which was the first result of the victory for the Union was the conduct of the South itself. Beaten in arms and impoverished, stripped of slavery, the white South found solace, or saw relief, if not recompense, in harsh treatment of the emancipated negroes, in laws, in business, and in social relations. The effect of this folly was decisive at the North. But added to this was the fatuous course of President Johnson, to whom the South, not unnaturally, gave warm support.

Out of these adverse conditions came reconstruction. Its inception and development into policy and law were not the results or dictates of sober judgment of what was best; least of all were they inspired by statesmanlike forecast, or the teachings of philosophy or history. The writer has recently turned over anew the congressional discussions, in 1866 and 1867, of reconstruction, the South, and especially the negro question, some large part of which he heard at first-hand. It is, for by far the greater part, melancholy reading—shocking in its crudeness and disregard of facts and actualities, amazing for the confident levity of tone on the part of the leading advocates of the reconstruction acts of 1867, and for its narrowly partisan spirit. Confidence here rose easily into prophecy, and the country was

assured of a peaceful, prosperous South, with negro loyalty forever at the helm. The white South was helpless. The black South
was equal to all the needs of the hour: ignorant, to be sure,
but loyal; inexperienced, but, with the ballot as its teacher and
inspiration, capable of assuring good government. Hardly anywhere else in recorded debates can be found so surprising a
revelation of the blindness of partisan zeal as these discussions
disclose. But it may now be clear to all, as it was then clear to
some, that underneath all the avowed motives and all the open
arguments lay a deeper cause than all others—the will and determination to secure party ascendency and control at the South
and in the nation through the negro vote. If this is a hard saying,
let any one now ask himself, or ask the public, if it is possibly
credible that the reconstruction acts would have been passed if
the negro vote had been believed to be Democratic.

True views of the situation—views sound, enlightened, and
statesmanlike—were not wanting even then. Mr. Lincoln had
presented such views; but above all other men in the whole land,
Governor Andrew, of Massachusetts, in his farewell address to
the Massachusetts legislature, January 2, 1866, discussed with
elaboration the Southern situation, and urged views and suggested policies which will mark him always in our annals, at
least with the highest minds, as a true, prescient, and lofty statesman, versed in the past and able to prejudge the future. His
valedictory address is veritably prophetic—as prophetic as it is
politic and practical. With this great word resounding through
the country, the last excuse for reconstruction as actually fixed
upon is swept away; for it could not longer be held, as it had
been said by the more timid or doubtful, that the whole business
was a groping in the dark, without light or leading. Sentiment
carried the day, sentiment of the lower kind—hate, revenge,
greed, lust of power.

It is, however, necessary at this point to be just. Not all who
bore part in fixing the terms of reconstruction were ignoble or

ignorant. Among them were many unselfish doctrinaires, humanitarians, and idealists of fine type. Among them, too, were men who ranked as statesmen, who in other fields had well earned the name, but who now were overborne or overpersuaded. Back of all these, however, were the party leaders, who moved on, driving the reluctant, crushing and ostracizing the doubtful, brutally riding down those who dared to oppose.

Governor Andrew's argument and policy may be briefly stated. Three great, flashing apothegms summarize it: (1) Prosecute peace as vigorously as we have prosecuted war. (2) Inflict no humiliation, require no humiliation, of the South. (3) Enlist the sympathy and services of "the natural leaders" of the South in the work of reconstruction. To the oft-repeated dictum that those who had ruled the South so long and rigorously—its natural leaders—could not be trusted with this work, Andrew pointed out, with prophetic insight, that these men, if not accepted as friends, would resume their leadership as enemies. Such a vision of the future, such a clear annunciation of truth and fact, fell on blind and impatient or angry minds. The most radical of antebellum and war Republicans, the greatest of all our war governors, was struck from the list of party leaders, and reconstruction proceeded apace on other lines and under other leaders. The writer recalls almost numberless interviews on reconstruction with Republican leaders at Washington, especially in the winter of 1866–67, and the summer and fall of the latter year, and particularly with the late Oliver P. Morton. Mr. Morton shared to some large degree with Mr. Thaddeus Stevens the leadership in this enterprise. Against the two combined, no policy could gain even consideration. With Mr. Stevens no argument was possible. His mind was fixed, proof against facts or reason that suggested other views. Mere personal self-respect limited the writer's intercourse with him to one brief conversation. Not one of these leaders had seen the South, or studied it at first-hand. Not one of them professed or cared to know more. They had made up their minds once for all, and they wished only to push on with their predetermined policy. The one descriptive feature, the one overshadowing item, of their policy was, as has been said, negro suffrage, loyalty under a black skin at the helm—a policy which, like other historical policies of "Thorough," like the policy of Strafford and Laud, whence the fitting word has come, brooked no opposition or delay, and halted for no arguments or obstacles whilst these leaders led. The personal knowledge of the writer warrants him in stating that eyes were never blinder to facts, minds never more ruthlessly set upon a policy, than were Stevens and Morton on putting the white South under the heel of the black South. Again it is necessary to say that not all eminent Republican leaders shared these sentiments, though they acquiesced in the policy. Mr. Sumner, it shall be said, did not, and, strange perhaps to add, Mr. Blaine did not; but both submitted, and even advocated the acts of 1867.

Reconstruction thus conceived, thus developed, thus expounded, was put to test in South Carolina in the winter of 1867–68. Passed, as these acts were, in lofty disregard of the feelings or interest of the whites of the South, the first crucial test they met was of course the attitude of those who were thus disregarded. The first force or element to be reckoned with was the element left out of the account. The property, the education and intelligence, the experience in self-government and public affairs, in this state, were of course wholly with its white population. Numbers alone were with the rest. The first registration of voters in South Carolina under the reconstruction acts, in October, 1867, gave a total of 125,328 persons eligible to vote, of whom 46,346 were whites, and 78,982 were blacks or colored, or a ratio of about 3 to 5. Upon the question of holding a constitutional convention, the first question prescribed by the acts for decision, the total vote in November, 1867, was 71,807—130 whites and 68,876 colored voting *pro*, and 2,801 *contra*. Of the members of the convention, 34 were whites and 63 colored. It did not contain one Democrat or one white man who had had high standing in the state previously. By this convention a constitution was framed, made up entirely of excerpts from other state constitutions, but yet a fairly good constitution in all its most important provisions. It continued in force, with a few rather unimportant changes, until 1897. State officers, under this constitution, and a legislature were elected in April, 1868, and the new government went into operation in July, 1868. In the first legislature under reconstruction, the Senate, numbering 33 members, contained 9 colored and 24 whites, of whom 7 only were Democrats. The House of Representatives numbered 124, of whom 48 were whites and 76 colored, only 14 being Democrats. The whole legislature was thus composed of 72 whites and 85 colored, with a total of 21 Democrats to 136 Republicans, or a ratio of nearly 3 to 20.

Truth here requires it to be said that the abstention of the whites from coöperation at this stage of reconstruction was voluntary and willful. The election for members of the convention went by default so far as they were concerned. They might, by voting solidly, and by the use of cajolery and flattery, such as they later did use, or by grosser arts, from which at last they did not shrink, have won an influential if not a controlling voice. All this is clear and certain; but the fact only shows the recklessness with which the sponsors of reconstruction went ahead. Such abnegation of lifelong sentiments or prejudices, such absolute reversal of themselves, as such a line of conduct required, was possible; but decent statesmanship does not build on possibilities. The question should have been, not, Is such conduct on the part of the whites possible? but, Is it to be expected? No man can say less than that it was to the last degree improbable; it would hardly be too much to say it was morally impossible. Alone of all prominent men in the state, Wade Hampton in 1868 publicly advised coöperation with the negroes in elections, but his advice passed unheeded.

But it is not true that Stevens or Morton counted on such co-öperation of the whites, or cared for it. It was an afterthought to claim it; a retort to those who uttered reproaches as the scheme of reconstruction gradually showed its vanity and impossibility. It cannot be too confidently asserted that from 1867 to 1872 nothing would have been more unwelcome to the leaders of reconstruction at Washington than the knowledge that the whites of South Carolina were gaining influence over the blacks, or were helping to make laws, or were holding office. The writer knows his ground here; and there is available written evidence in abundance to avouch all his statements and opinions—evidence, too, which will sometime be given to the world.

No view of the situation in South Carolina in these years would be accurate or complete which did not call to mind the peculiar political or party condition of the white or Democratic population. For fully ten years, if not twenty, prior to 1850, Mr. Calhoun's immense personality, strenuous leadership, and unquestionably representative views and policies dominated the state—dominated it to the complete effacement and disappearance of all other leaders or leadership. This influence projected itself forward, and controlled the thought of the state until 1860, as truly as in the lifetime of Calhoun. American political history, for its first century, will record no other instance of individual supremacy over a high-spirited, ambitious, politics-loving community such as the career of Calhoun presents. Nor was his influence in the smallest degree factitious or adventitious. It was simply the result of the application of a stern will, prodigious industry, sleepless but not selfish ambition, and the very highest order of ability to the leadership of a political cause. Calhoun led South Carolina till the outbreak of the war, if not through the war. At the close of the war and at the date of the reconstruction acts, new leadership in political thought and action was necessary; but South Carolina then had no leaders. Not only had she no trained party or political leaders; she had no men of single commanding influence. The most influential men of the state were the heroes of the war, who, though many of them able and public-spirited, were none of them greatly experienced in public affairs. The state had its full share of able men, an especially able bar, great numbers of planters and business men who had the old-time training in politics, but no man who could to any great degree mould public opinion or control party action. This fact—and it is referred to here only as a fact—was significant of much. In consequence, the Democratic or white party merely drifted, rudderless and at haphazard, from 1867 to 1874, the critical years of reconstruction.

Here, as at all points in this paper, the writer intends to speak with moderation of spirit and entire frankness. He thinks he can do justice to all parties and persons who took active part in reconstruction, though himself an actor, at times somewhat prominent. It will be for others to judge whether he has succeeded, as he has tried to do, in laying aside prejudices or feelings naturally developed by his activity in these scenes, so that he can see the men and events of those days objectively and disinterestedly.

It is now plain to all that reconstruction under the acts of 1867 was, at any rate, a frightful experiment, which never could have given a real statesman who learned or knew the facts the smallest hope of success. Government, self-government, the care of common public interests by the people themselves, is not so easy or simple a task as not to require a modicum of experience as well as a modicum of mental and moral character. In the mass of 78,000 colored voters in South Carolina in 1867, what elements or forces could have existed that made for good government? Ought it not to have been as clear then as it is now that good government, or even tolerable administration, could not be had from such an aggregation of ignorance and inexperience and incapacity? Is it not, has it not always been, as true in government as in physics, *ex nihilo nihil fit?*

Added to this obvious discouragement and impossibility in South Carolina was the fact that these 78,000 colored voters were distinctly and of design pitted against 46,000 whites, who held all the property, education, and public experience of the state. It is not less than shocking to think of such odds, such inveitable disaster. Yet it was deliberately planned and eagerly welcomed at Washington, and calmly accepted by the party throughout the country. What Republican voice was heard against it?

But the cup of adverse conditions was not yet full. To this feast of reconstruction, this dance of reunion, rushed hundreds, even thousands, of white and colored men from the North, who had almost as little experience of public affairs as the negroes of the South; and it must be added that, as a class, they were not morally the equals of the negroes of the South. The story at this point is threadbare; but it must be again said in this review that the Northern adventurers at once sprang to the front, and kept to the front from 1867 to 1874. To them the negro deferred with a natural docility. He felt that they represented the powers at Washington, as they often did, and his obedience was easily se-cured and held. Are Stevens and Morton and their applauding supporters chargeable with counternancing these men? Not by express, direct terms; but they are justly chargeable with open-ing the doors to them, and not casting them off when their true character was perfectly known. So ingrained was the disregard of Southern Democrats in all affairs that concerned the political control at the South, so inflexible was the determination of offi-cials and leaders at Washington to keep the heel on the neck, that hardly one high Republican authority could be appealed to for discountenance of the class referred to. To this tide of folly, and worse, President Grant persistently yielded; while one noble ex-ception must be noted, the gallant and true Benjamin H. Bristow, of Kentucky, as Solicitor-General, Attorney-General, and Sec-retary of the Treasury.

The quick, sure result was of course misgovernment. Let a few statistics tell the tale. Before the war, the average expense of the annual session of the legislature in South Carolina did not exceed $20,000. For the six years following reconstruction the average annual expense was over $320,000, the expense of the session of 1871 alone being $617,000. The total legislative expenses for the six years were $2,339,000.

The average annual cost of public printing in Massachusetts for the last ten years has been $131,000; for the year 1899 it was $139,000, and this included much costly printing never dreamed of in South Carolina in those days. In reconstructed South Caroline the cost of public printing for the first six years was $1,104,000—an annual average of $184,000, the cost for the single year 1871–72 being $348,000.

The total public debt of South Carolina at the beginning of reconstruction was less than $1,000,000. At the end of the year 1872, five years later, the direct public debt amounted to over $17,500,000. For all this increase the state had not a single public improvement of any sort to show; and of this debt over $5,950,000 had been formally repudiated by the party and the men who had created the debt, and received and handled its proceeds.

Prior to reconstruction, contingent funds were absolutely unknown in South Carolina; a contingent fund, as known under reconstruction, being a sum of money which a public officer was allowed to draw and expend without accountability. During the first six years of reconstruction the contingent funds in South Carolina amounted to $376,000.

These are pecuniary results, but they tell a moral tale. No such results could be possible except where public and private virtue was well-nigh extinct; nor could they exist alone. In fact, they were only one salient effect or phase of a wide reign of corruption and general misrule. Public offices were objects of vulgar, commonplace bargain and sale. Justice in the lower and higher courts was bought and sold; or rather, those who sat in the seats nominally of justice made traffic of their judicial powers. State militia on a vast scale was organized and equipped in 1870 and 1871 solely from the negroes, arms and legal organization being denied the white Democrats. No branch of the public service escaped the pollution. One typical and concrete example must suffice here. In the counties of South Carolina there is a school commissioner whose powers and duties cover the choice of all teachers of the public schools, their examination for employment or promotion, the issue of warrants for installments of their salary, and, in general, all the powers and duties usually devolved on the highest school officer in a given area of territory. In one of the counties of South Carolina, during the years 1874 and 1875, the school commissioner was a negro of the deepest hue and most pronounced type, who could neither read nor write even his own name; and his name appeared always on official documents in another's handwriting, with the legend "his x mark." He was as corrupt, too, as he was ignorant. Now, what course a county in Massachusetts or other Northern state would take under such an infliction the writer does not venture to say. He is only certain no Northern community would stand it. The people of this county, one morning, found their chief school officer dead in the highway from a gunshot. Such incidents must lead, will lead, in any intelligent community, to deeds of violence. The famous and infamous Kuklux Klan of 1870 was an organized attempt to over-awe and drive from office Republican state officers, and especially negroes. It was brutal and murderous to the last degree, being from first to last in the hands almost exclusively of the lower stratum of the white population. Yet it was symptomatic of a dreadful disease—the gangrene of incapacity, dishonesty, and corruption in public office. No excuse can be framed for its outrages, but its causes were plain. Any observer who cared to see could see that it flourished where corruption and incapacity had climbed into power, and withered where the reverse was the case.

Gradually, under the spur of public wrongs and misrule, political party remedies began to be used by the Democrats—a word practically synonymous with whites, as Republican was with negroes—and in 1872 a Democratic canvass was made for state officers. In 1874 the Democrats united with a section of disaffected Republicans in a canvass, in which the Republican candidate for governor received 80,000 votes, and the Democratic candidate 68,000. Still no great or preëminent leader of the Democratic party forces had appeared. In 1874, under the stress of fear of consequences, symptoms of which were then clear, the Republican party, by some of its leaders, and some part of its rank and file, undertook a somewhat systematic effort for "reform within the party." For the next two years the struggle went determinedly on, with varying success. Two facts or incidents will illustrate the flow and ebb of reform here. Early in 1875, a notorious, corrupt negro, who had long led the negroes in one of the strongest Republican sections of the state, put himself up as a candidate for judge of the chief (Charleston) circuit of the state. The reform forces barely succeeded in defeating him. Other conflicts from time to time arose, and it was only by a close union of the Democrats in the legislature, and the free and constant use of the executive power of veto, that the reform party was saved from overthrow and rout—no less than nineteen vetoes being given to leading legislative measures by the governor in a single session. When the legislature assembled for the session of 1875–76, the reform and anti-reform forces were nearly equally matched; the former including all the Democratic members of the legislature, who were in turn heartily backed by the Democratic party of the state.

A decisive test of strength soon came. As the event of this test marks accurately the turning point in the fortunes of reconstruction in South Carolina under the congressional plan of 1867, the story must be here told with care and some degree of fullness. December 15, 1875, occurred an election by the legislature of six

circuit or *nisi prius* judges for the several circuits into which the
state was then divided. On the night preceding the election a
secret caucus of the negro members of the legislature was held,
instigated, organized, and led by the most adroit as well as the
ablest negro in the state, one Robert B. Elliott, formerly of Boston. At this caucus, an oath was sworn by every member to support all nominations made by the caucus for the judgeships.
The caucus proceeded to make nominations, choosing for the
two most important circuits—Charleston and Sumter—a negro,
Whipper, and a white man, F. J. Moses. Not till the legislature
was ready to meet on the following day did the fact of this caucus become known. Every man nominated was elected. The
storm now broke over the heads of the conspirators in fury. The
laugh which for a long time greeted remonstrance died away,
and men asked one another what could be done. The governor at
once took his stand, undoubtedly a novel and extreme stand; but,
like all decent men who saw the situation at first-hand, he probably felt that sometimes in politics, as in other things, "new occasions teach new duties." He publicly announced his determination to refuse to issue commissions to Whipper and Moses.
The wrath of the conspirators rose high, but the white citizens
strongly backed the executive, and no commissions were ever
issued. The sequel was that, after much loud boasting of their
courage on the part of Whipper and Moses, they quailed, like
the craven cowards they were, before the determination of the
people, and never took another step to enforce their claim to
office.

At this precise point came the parting of ways between the
governor and his Republican supporters, on the one hand, and
his white Democratic supporters, on the other hand, in their
common reform struggle. It seems dramatic, almost tragic, that,
in a matter of so much importance to South Carolina, hearts
equally earnest and honest, as we may now believe, and minds
equally free and clear, saw in the same event, and that event a

signal triumph over the powers of misrule by the allied forces of the reformers, totally different meanings and significance. To the Republican reformers it seemed a splendid vindication of their policy and belief—that all that was needed was a union of the forces of intelligence and honesty against the common enemy; to the Democratic reformers, on the other hand, it seemed a final and crowning proof that the forces of misrule were too strong to be overcome by ordinary, peaceful methods. Less cannot be said here than that, as is usual, there was truth in both views. There were, no doubt, many searchings of heart in the ranks of each division of the reformers. One eminent and devoted reformer, who felt compelled to go with the Democrats, has left on record an expression of his feelings, in quoting the words of Sir William Waller to his friend and antagonist in the English Civil War of 1640: "That great God who is the searcher of my heart knows with what a sad sense I go upon this service, and with what a perfect hatred I detest this war without an enemy. . . . But we are both upon the stage, and must act such parts as are assigned us in this tragedy." It was the feeling of many before the contest had opened or passed to the stage of hard fighting.

Pause must be made here long enough to set before an uninformed reader the array of forces for this contest, so significant to South Carolina, and so characteristic and illustrative of the inevitable results of reconstruction on the lines of 1876. It has been remarked that South Carolina had no great leader or leaders after Mr. Calhoun. This was true until 1876, but not later. Great new occasions usually bring leaders. At the head of the Democratic forces in South Carolina, in June, 1876, appeared General Wade Hampton, known only, one might say, till then, except locally, as a distinguished Confederate cavalry officer. He had led the life of a planter on a large scale, and possessed well-developed powers and habits of command. Totally unlike Calhoun, Hampton's strength of leadership lay, not in intellectual or oratorical superiority, but in high and forceful character, perfect courage, and real devotion to what he conceived to be the welfare of South Carolina. Not even Calhoun's leadership was at any time more absolute, unquestioned, and enthusiastic than Hampton's in 1876; and it was justly so from the Democratic point of view, for he was unselfish, resolute, level-headed, and determined. He was for the hour a true "natural leader"; and he led with consummate mingled prudence and aggressiveness.

The progress of the canvass developed, as must have been apprehended by all who saw or studied the situation, not only into violence of words and manner, but into breaches of the peace, interference with public meetings called by one party, and latterly into widespread riots. The chapter need not be retold. The concealments of the canvass on these points have long been remitted, with the occasion which called for them. It is not now denied, but admitted and claimed, by the successful party, that the canvass was systematically conducted with the view to find occasions to apply force and violence. The occasions came, and the methods adopted had their perfect work. The result is known, but must be stated here for historical purposes purely. By a system of violence and coercion ranging through all possible grades, from urgent persuasion to mob violence and plentiful murders, the election was won by the Democrats. The historian here is no longer compelled to spell out his verdict from a wide induction of facts; he need only accept the assertions, even the vaunts, of many of the leading figures in the canvass since the canvass was closed.

Is there anything to be said by way of verdict upon the whole passage? Yes; plainly this, at least—that the drama or tragedy lay potentially, from the first, in the reconstruction policy of Morton and Stevens. The latent fire there concealed was blown to flame by the conduct of affairs in South Carolina under the inspiration, if not direction, of Republican leaders at Washington. No proper or serious efforts were ever made there to ward off or prevent the conflict. Till October, 1876, no doubt seemed to enter the minds of Republican politicians that the brute force of numbers would win, as it had won. Cries of distress, shouts of encouragement, promises of reward for the party in South Carolina, now burdened the mails and kept telegraph wires hot. Managers of the Republican national canvass vied with one another in the extravagance of hopes and promises sent to South Carolina. But the forces aroused by ten years of vassalage of white to black, and eight years of corruption and plunder and misrule, moved on to their end till the end was fully reached.

It has often been asked, Could not the end—freedom from negro domination and its consequent misrule—have been reached by other more lawful and more peaceful methods? Into speculations of this kind it is not worth while to venture. One thing may be said with confidence—the whites of South Carolina in 1876 believed no other methods or means would avail. Their course was guided by this belief. Mr. Hallam declares that "nothing is more necessary, in reaching historical conclusions, than knowledge of the motives avowed and apparently effective in the minds of the parties to controversies." The avowed motives of the whites in the struggle of 1876 are fully recorded. Are there any evidences that these motives were simulated or affected? The policy adopted and carried out does not discredit the existence and force of these motives. The campaign of 1876 was conducted as if it were a life-or-death combat.

Finally, the more serious, most serious, question has often been raised: Conceding the wrongs suffered and the hopelessness of relief by other methods, was this campaign warranted? Different answers will be given by different moralists and casuists. To the writer, the question does not seem of first or great importance. What is certain is that a people of force, pride, and intelligence, driven, as the white people of South Carolina believed they were in 1876, to choose between violence and lawlessness for a time, and misrule for all time, will infallibly choose the former.

The overthrow of Republican or negro rule in South Carolina in 1876 was root-and-branch work. The fabric so long and laboriously built up fell in a day. Where was fancied to be strength was found only weakness. The vauntings were turned to cringings of terror. Poltroons and perjurers made haste to confess; robbers came forward to disgorge, intent only on personal safety; and the world saw an old phenomenon repeated—the essential and ineradicable cowardice and servility of conscious wrongdoers. The avalanche caught the innocent with the guilty, the patriot and reformer with the corruptionist, the bribe giver and bribe taker. It could not be otherwise; it has never been otherwise in such convulsions.

The historian who studies this crowning event of reconstruction in South Carolina will be sure to meet or to raise the question, Why did Republican reformers there adhere to the Republican party in 1876? The answer to this is easy. They were, most of them, trained in another school than South Carolina. Resort to violence and bloodshed was not in their list of possible remedies for political wrongs or abuses. They were ready to risk or to lose their own lives in a contest for good government; they were not ready to take the lives or shed the blood of others for any political cause not involving actual physical self-defense.

A close or interested student of reconstruction will doubtless ask, In the light of retrospect and the disillusionment of later events, does it seem that good government could have been reached in South Carolina by a continuance of the union of a part—the reforming part—of the Republican party and the whole body of Democrats in the state? Speculation and reflection have been and will be expended on this question, for to some degree it touches a vital moral point. It has already been said that on this question the two wings—Republican and Democratic—of the reformers of 1874–76 held opposite opinions. It must be conceded that, unfortunately but inevitably, into the decision of the question in 1876 purely party considerations entered strongly. It would be vain for either side to deny it. Republican reformers were party men; so were Democratic reformers. Personal ambitions, also, played their usual part—a large one. Instigations to a strict Republican party contest came freely from Washington. On the other hand, Mr. Tilden, who was made to bear in those days so heavy a load of responsibility for everything amiss in the eyes of his party opponents, was specially charged—a charge still current among the uninformed or the victims of ancient party prejudices—with influencing the Democratic party in South Carolina in this crisis to enter on a party canvass on the lines of violence and fraud. The writer thinks he now knows the charge to be unfounded; that, on the contrary, if Mr. Tilden's influence was felt at all, it was in the direction of a canvass for state officers and the legislature on non-partisan lines, and in any event a peaceful and lawful canvass. If there is any interest still attaching to the writer's own view, he is quite ready now to say that he feels sure there was no possibility of securing permanent good government in South Carolina through Republican influences. If the canvass of 1876 had resulted in the success of the Republican party, that party could not, for want of materials, even when aided by the Democratic minority, have given pure or competent administration. The vast preponderance of ignorance and incapacity in that party, aside from downright dishonesty, made it impossible. An experienced or observant eye can see the causes. The canvass on purely party lines in 1876 necessarily threw Republican reformers and Republican rascals again into friendly contact and alliance. Success would have given redoubled power to leaders who had been temporarily discredited or set aside; the flood gates of misrule would have been reopened; and, as was said by one of the leaders of reform when Whipper and Moses were elected judges, "a terrible crevasse of misgovernment and public debauchery" would have again opened. The real truth is, hard as it may be to accept it, that the elements put in combination by the reconstruction scheme of Stevens and Morton were irretrievably bad, and could never have resulted, except temporarily or in desperate moments, in government fit to be endured. As Macaulay's old Puritan sang in after years of Naseby, so may now sing a veteran survivor of reconstruction in South Carolina:

> Oh! evil was the root, and bitter was the fruit,
> And crimson was the juice of the vintage that we trod.

There is an important inquiry still to be noticed and answered: How did the victors use their victory? The just answer seems to be, "Not altogether well," but emphatically, "As well as could have been expected"—as well as the lot and nature of humanity probably permit. Some unfair, unjust, merely angry blows were struck after the victory was won. For the rest, forbearance and oblivion were the rule. Good government, the avowed aim, was fully secured. Economy succeeded extravagance; judicial integrity and ability succeeded profligacy and ignorance on the bench; all the conditions of public welfare were restored.

Of secondary results, it is hardly necessary to this review and picture of reconstruction in South Carolina to speak; but it would be an impressive warning for other like cases if it were added that the methods of 1876 have left scars and wounds which generations of time cannot efface or heal. The appeal for the truth of this remark may be safely made to the most ardent defender of those methods. The price of what was gained in 1876 will long remain unliquidated. No part of it can ever be remitted. The laws of human society, not written in statute books, proclaim that wrong and wrong methods are self-propagating. Long before Shakespeare told it, it was true, even from the foundation of the moral order:

> We but teach
> Bloody instructions, which being taught, return
> To plague the inventor; this even-handed justice
> Commends the ingredients of our poison'd chalice
> To our own lips.

Every present citizen of South Carolina knows, and those who are truthful and frank will confess, that the ballot debauched in 1876 remains debauched; the violence taught then remains now, if not in the same, in other forms; the defiance of law learned then in what was called a good cause survives in the horrid orgies and degradation of lynchings.

The chapter of recent events covered by this paper is made up largely of the record of mistakes and crimes followed by the sure, unvarying retributions which all history teaches are the early or late result of evil courses in nations and states as well as in individuals. To whom, humanly speaking, are these woes and wastes chargeable? The answer must be, to those who devised and put in operation the congressional scheme of reconstruction—to their unspeakable folly, their blind party greed, their insensate attempt to reverse the laws which control human society.

The designed plan of this paper does not extend to any discussion of the always grave topic of the condition and prospects of the negro race in South Carolina and the South. It has abundantly appeared in what has already been written that that race was used as the tool of heartless partisan leaders. As in all such cases, the tool was cast aside when its use was ended. Who can look on the picture—the negro enslaved by physical chains for some two centuries and a half, then bodily lifted into freedom by other hands than his own, next mercilessly exploited for the benefit of a political party, and heartlessly abandoned when the scheme had failed—what heart of stone, we say, would not be touched by these undeserved miseries, these woeful misfortunes, of the negro of the United States?

What had the negro to show after 1876 for his sufferings? Merely the paper right to vote—a right which he had no earthly power or capacity to use or to defend; while, with smug faces, with hypocritic sighs and upturned eyeballs, the *soi-distant* philanthropists and charitymongers of the North looked on the negro from afar, giving him only an occasional charge to still stand by the grand old party that had set him free! To all who feel a real solicitude for the welfare of the Southern negro, it ought to be said that the conditions of his welfare lie in reversing at all points the spirit and policy of reconstruction which brought on him this Iliad of woes. Philanthropy without wisdom is always dangerous. Disregard of actual conditions is never wise. The negro depends for his welfare, not on the North, but on the South; not on strangers, however friendly or sympathetic or generous in bestowing bounty, but on his white neighbors and employers. Whatever can be done to promote good relations between him and his actual neighbors will be well done; whatever is done which tends otherwise will be ill done. By industry and thrift the negro can secure all he needs, both of livelihood and of education; whatever is given him gratuitously promotes idleness and unthrift. With all emphasis let it be said and known—and the writer's knowledge confirms the saying, as will like knowledge acquired by any honest and clear-sighted person—that the negro at the South is not, in the mass or individually, the proper object of charity.

And of his education let a word be said. Education is, no one disputes or doubts, essential to the welfare of a free or self-governing community. The negro in his present situation is not an exception to the rule. But what sort of education does he need? Primarily, and in nine hundred and ninety-nine cases out of one thousand, he does not need, in any proper sense of the words, literary, scientific, or what we call the higher education. It is not too much to say that, up to this time, a great amount of money and effort has been worse than wasted on such education, or attempts at such education, of the negro. To an appreciable extent, it has been a positive evil to him. Give him, or rather stimulate him to provide for himself, education suited to his condition: to wit, abundant training in the three R's; and after that, skill in handicraft, in simple manual labor of all kinds, which it is his lot to do—lot fixed not by us, but by powers above us. If there be aspiring spirits in the race, capable of better things, this is the soil from which they may rise, rather than from hotbeds or forcing grounds—the so-called negro colleges and universities now existing in the South. Beyond this, let the negro be taught, early and late, in schools and everywhere, thrift, pecuniary prudence and foresight, the duty, the foremost duty, of getting homes, property, land, or whatever constitutes wealth in his community. Above all things, let him be taught that his so-called rights depend on himself alone. Tell him, compel him by iteration to know, that no race or people has ever yet long had freedom unless it was won and kept by itself; won and kept by courage, by intelligence, by vigilance, by prudence. Having done this, let Northern purses be closed; let sympathy and bounty be bestowed, if anywhere, upon far less favored toilers nearer home, and leave the negro to work out his own welfare, unhelped and unhindered. If these simple methods are adopted and rigorously observed, the negro problem at our South will tend toward solution, and the flood of ills flowing from reconstruction as imposed from without will at last be stayed; and they can be stayed in no other ways. Constitutional limits of aid by legislation have already been reached and overpassed. Rights, to be secure, must, in the last resort, rest on stronger supports than constitutions, statutes, or enrolled parchments. Self-government under constitutions presupposes a firm determination, and mental, moral and physical capacity, ready and equal to the defense of rights. Neither the negro nor the white man can have them on other terms.

The Ku Klux Movement

WILLIAM GARROTT BROWN

Whoever can remember Mr. Edwin Booth in the character of Richelieu will doubtless recall his expression of the sudden change which comes over the melodramatic cardinal toward the end of the scene in which his house is invaded by the conspirators. While he is ignorant of his danger, his helplessness in the grasp of his swarming enemies, Richelieu is all majesty, all tragedy. But when he learns that every avenue of escape is barred, that even Huguet is false, that no open force will avail him, his towering mood gives place, not indeed to any cringing fear, but to subtlety and swift contriving. His eyes no longer blaze, but twinkle; his finger is at his chin; there is a semblance of a grin about his lips.

> All? Then the lion's skin's too short tonight,—
> Now for the fox's.

The simulated deathbed follows. The enemy, too powerful to be resisted, is outwitted and befooled.

Twenty-five years ago, when a negro inquired of his former master about "dem Ku Kluxes," the response he got was awe-inspiring. If a child of the household made the same inquiry of his elders, his question was put away with an unsatisfying answer and a look like Mr. Booth's in the play. Had the great cardinal lived south of Mason and Dixon's line in the late sixties, I fancy he would have found the Ku Klux Klan an instrument altogether to his liking.

The Southern child who, not content with the grin and the evasive answer of his father or his elder brother, sought further enlightenment from his fast friends of the kitchen and the quarters, heard such stories of the mysterious, sheeted brotherhood as eclipsed in his young fancy even the entrancing rivalry of Brer Fox and Brer Rabbit, and made the journey back to the "big house" at bedtime a terrifying experience. Uncle Lewis would tell of a shrouded horseman who rode silently up to his door at midnight, begged a drink of water, and tossed off a whole bucketful at a draught. Uncle Lewis was sure he could hear it sizzling as it flowed down that monstrous gullet, and readily accepted the stranger's explanation that it was the first drop he had tasted since he was killed at Shiloh. Aunt Lou, coming home from the house of a neighboring auntie who was ill, and crossing a lonesome stretch near the graveyard, had distinctly seen a group of horsemen, motionless by the roadside, each with his head in his hand. Alec, a young mulatto who had once shown much interest in politics, had been stopped on his way from a meeting of his " 'ciety" by a masked horseman, at least eight feet tall, who insisted upon shaking hands; and when Alec grasped his hand, it was the hand of a skeleton. Darkies who, unlike Uncle Lewis and Aunt Lou and Alec, had turned against their own white people and taken up with the Yankees, had been more roughly handled.

Somehow, in one such Southern boy's memories there is always a dim association of these Ku Klux stories with other stories of the older negroes about "patterrollers." Through them all there jingles the refrain,

> Run, nigger, run!
> De patterrollers ketch you.

When that boy went to college and joined a society that had initiations, the mystery and horror of the Ku Klux stories waned; but it was not until he read an account of the patrol system of slavery times that he saw the connection between Ku Klux and "patterrollers."

An organization that could so mystify all but the grown-up white men of a Southern household certainly lost none of its mystery in the confused accounts that filled the newspapers of that day, and citizens of the Northern states, already tired of the everlasting Southern question, could not be expected to understand it. Congress, when it undertook to enlighten them, swelled its records with much impassioned oratory, and through its committees of investigation put into print first one and then thirteen bulky volumes, from which he who lives long enough to read it all may learn much that is true but not particularly important, much that is important if true, and somewhat that is both true and important. From the mass of it the Republican majority got matter sufficient to sustain one set of conclusions, leaving unused enough to sustain quite as strongly the entirely different conclusions at which the minority arrived. There remained much upon which American novelists, whether humorously or sensationally inclined, have drawn, and may continue to draw. Dr. Conan Doyle, seeking to "paint a horror skillfully," found the Klan a good nerveracker, though it is to be hoped he did not attempt to digest the reports. Voluminous as they are, they need to be supplemented with material of a different sort—with such memories as the child of Reconstruction times can summon up, with such written memoranda and cautious talk as can be won from Southerners of an older generation, with such insight as one can get into Southern character and habits of thought and life—before one can begin to understand what the Klan was, or how it came into existence, or what its part was in that great confusion officially styled the Reconstruction of the Southern states.

Without attempting any elaborate argument, we may, I think, take it for granted that the Ku Klux movement was an outcome of the conditions that prevailed in the Southern states after the war. It was too widespread, too spontaneous, too clearly a popular movement, to be attributed to any one man or to any conspiracy of a few men. Had it existed only in one corner of the South, or drawn its membership from a small and sharply defined class, some such explanation might serve. But we know enough of its extent, its composition, and the various forms it took, to feel sure that it was neither an accident nor a scheme. It was no man's contrivance, but an historical development. As such, it must be studied against its proper background of a disordered society and a bewildered people. Various elements of the disorder and causes of the bewilderment have been set forth in the previous papers of this series. It will be necessary here to emphasize only one feature of the general misgovernment; namely, that the evil was by no means confined to the state governments, where the bolder adventurers and the more stupendous blunderers were at work. The itching and galling of the yoke was worst in the lesser communities, where government touches the lives of individual men and women most intimately.

The mismanagement—to use the mildest word—of state finances can be shown in figures with reasonable clearness. The oppression of counties and towns and school districts is less easily exhibited, though it was in this way the heaviest burdens of taxation were imposed. The total increase in the indebtedness of the smaller political units under carpet-bag rule was, as a matter of fact, even greater than in the case of the state governments; and the wrong was done in plainer view of the taxpayer, by acts more openly and vulgarly tyrannical. So far as the tax-payer's feelings were concerned, piling up state debts had the effect which the mismanagement of a bank has on the stock-holders. The piling up of county and town and school taxes was like thrusting hands visibly and forcibly into his pockets. It is doubtful, however, if even the injury to his fortunes had so much to do with his state of mind as the countless humiliations and irritations which the rule of the freedman and the stranger brought upon the most imperious, proud, and sensitive branch of the English race.

If the white man of the lately dominant class in the South were permitted to vote at all, he might have literally to pass under bayonets to reach the polls. He saw freedmen organized in militia companies, expensively armed and gayly caparisoned. If he offered his own military services, they were sure to be rejected. He saw his former slaves repeating at elections, but he learned that he had no right of challenge, and that there was no penalty fixed by law for the crime. In the local courts of justice, he saw his friends brought, by an odious system of informers, before judges who were not merely incompetent or unfair, like many of those who sat in the higher courts, but often gro-tesquely ignorant as well, and who intrusted the execution of their instruments to officials who in many cases could not write an intelligible return. In the schools which he was so heavily taxed to support, he saw the children of his slaves getting the book learning which he himself thought it unwise to give them from strangers who would be sure to train them into discontent with the only lot he thought them fit for, and the only sort of work which, in the world he knew, they ever had a chance to do. He saw the Freedmen's Bureau deliberately trying to substitute its alien machinery for that patriarchal relation between white employers and black workmen which had seemed to him right and inevitable. He saw the Loyal League urging freedmen to take up those citizenly powers and duties which he had never understood emancipation to imply, when he gave up his sword. In every boisterous shout of a drunken negro before his gate, in every insolent glance from a group of idle negroes on the streets of the county seat, in the reports of fisticuffs with little darkies which his children brought home after school, in the noises of the night and the glare of occasional conflagrations, he saw the hand or heard the harshly accented voice of the stranger in the land. The biographer of the late Justice Lamar makes a picture which might convey to the reader some idea of the inevitable effect of these things on such men as the Southerners of those days were. It is a picture of the distinguished orator leaning over the ruinous fence in front of his home in a little Mississippi town, hatless, coatless, the great mass of his hair and beard neglected, returning with a surly nod the greetings of his acquaintance.

It seems astounding, nowadays, that the congressional leaders in reconstruction did not foresee that men of their own stock, so circumstanced, would resist, and would find some means to make their resistance effective. When they did make up their minds to resist—not collectively or through any representative body, but singly and by neighborhoods—they found an instrument ready to their hands.

When the Civil War ended, the little town of Pulaski, Tennessee, welcomed home a band of young men who, though they were veterans of hard-fought fields, were for the most part no older than the mass of college students. In the general poverty, the exhaustion, the lack of heart, naturally prevalent throughout the beaten South, young men had more leisure than was good for them. A Southern country town, even in the halcyon days before the war, was not a particularly lively place; and Pulaski in 1866 was doubtless rather tame to fellows who had seen Pickett charge at Gettysburg or galloped over the country with Morgan and Wheeler. A group of them, assembled in a law office one evening in May, 1866, were discussing ways and means of having a livelier time. Some one suggested a club or society. An organization with no very definite aims was effected; and at a second meeting, a week later, names were proposed and discussed. Some one pronounced the Greek word "Kuklos," meaning a circle. From "Kuklos" to "Ku Klux" was an easy transition—whoever consults a glossary of college boys' slang will not find it strange —and "Klan" followed "Ku Klux" as naturally as "dumpty" follows "humpty." That the name meant nothing whatever was a recommendation; and one can fancy what sort of badinage would have greeted a suggestion that in six years a committee of Congress would devote thirteen volumes to the history of the movement that began in a Pulaski law office, and migrated later to a deserted and half-ruined house on the outskirts of the village.

In the beginning it was, in fact, no "movement" at all. It was a scheme for having fun, more like a college secret society than anything else. Its members were not "lewd fellows of the baser sort," but young men of standing in the community, who a few years earlier would also have been men of wealth. The main source of amusement was at first the initiation of new members, but later the puzzling of outsiders. The only important clause in the oath of membership was a promise of absolute secrecy. The disguise was a white mask, a tall cardboard hat, a gown or robe that covered the whole person, and, when the Klan went mounted, a cover for the horses' bodies and some sort of muffling for their feet. The chief officers were a Grand Cyclops, or president; a Grand Magi, or vice president; a Grand Turk, or marshal; a Grand Exchequer, or treasurer; and two Lictors. While the club adhered to its original aim and character, only men of known good morals were admitted. Born of the same instinct and conditions that gave birth to the "snipe hunt" and other hazing deivces of Southern country towns, it was probably as harmless and as unimportant a piece of fooling as any to be found inside or outside of colleges.

The Klan was eminently successful. It got all the notoriety it wished, and very soon the youth of neighboring communities began to organize "dens" of their own. The mysterious features of the Klan were most impressive in rural neighborhoods. It spread rapidly in country districts. Probably it would have become a permanent secret society, not unlike the better known of the unserious secret societies now existing, but for the state of Southern politics and the progress of reconstruction. These things, however, soon gave a tremendous importance to the Klan's inevitable discovery that mystery and fear have over the African mind twice the power they have over the mind of a white man. It was not the first time in history that what began in mere purposeless fooling ended in the most serious way. By the time Congress had thrown aside the gentle and kindly plan of reconstruction, which Lincoln conceived and Johnson could not carry out, the Ku Klux had taught the white men of Tennessee and neighboring states the power of secrecy over the credulous race which Congress was bent on intrusting with the most difficult tasks of citizenship. When Southern society, turned upside down, groped about for some means of righting itself, it grasped the Pulaski idea.

As it happened, Tennessee, the original home of the Klan, was the very state in which reconstruction began earliest; and though the process there was somewhat different from the experience of the cotton states, it was also the first state to find its social and governmental systems upside down. Tennessee was notable for its large Unionist population. The Unionists were strongest in the mountainous eastern half of the state, while the western half, dominant before the war, was strongly secessionist. The first step in reconstruction was to put the east Tennesseeans into power; and the leader of the east Tennessee Unionists was "Parson" Brownlow. Except for his Unionism, Brownlow is generally conceded to have been an extremely unfit man for great public responsibilities, and when he became governor the secessionists of Tennessee had to endure much the same sort of misgovernment which in other states was attributable to carpet-bag offi-

187 1

cials. By the time it was a year old the Klan had gradually developed into a society of regulators, using its accidental machinery and its accidentally discovered power chiefly to suppress the lawlessness into which white men of Brownlow's following were sometimes led by their long-nourished grudge against their former rulers, and into which freedmen fell so inevitably that no fair-minded historian can mete out to them the full measure of censure for it. In the Union League the Klan found its natural enemy; and it is quite probably true that, during the early period of their rivalry for control, more inexcusable violence proceeded from the League than from the Klan.

However, a survivor and historian of the Klan does not deny that even thus early the abuses inseparable from secrecy existed in the order. To suppress them, and to adapt the order to its new and serious work, a convention was held at Nashville early in 1867. The Klan, up to that time bound together only by a general deference to the Grand Cyclops of the Pulaski "Den," was organized into the "Invisible Empire of the South," ruled by a Grand Wizard of the whole Empire, a Grand Dragon of each Realm, or state, a Grand Titan of each Dominion (Province), or county, a Grand Cyclops of each Den, and staff officers with names equally terrifying. The objects of the Klan, now that it had serious objects, were defined: they were to protect the people from indignities and wrongs; to succor the suffering, particularly the families of dead Confederate soldiers; to defend "the Constitution of the United States, and all laws passed in conformity thereto," and of the states also; and to aid in executing all constitutional laws, and protect the people from unlawful seizures and from trial otherwise than by jury. Acts of the Brownlow legislature reviving the alien and sedition laws were particularly held in mind.

From this time the Klan put itself more clearly in evidence, generally adhering to its original devices of mystery and silence, but not always successfully resisting the temptation to add to these violence. On the night of July 4, by well-heralded parades, it exhibited itself throughout Tennessee, and perhaps in other states, more impressively than ever before. In Pulaski, some four hundred disguised horsemen marched and countermarched silently through the streets before thousands of spectators, and not a single disguise was penetrated. The effect of mystery even on intelligent minds was well illustrated in the estimate, made by "reputable citizens," that the number was not less than three thousand. Members who lived in the town averted suspicion from themselves by appearing undisguised among the spectators. A gentleman who prided himself on knowing every horse in the county attempted to identify one by lifting its robe, and discovered that the animal and the saddle were his own!

The remaining facts in the history of the Ku Klux proper need no lengthy recital. The effectiveness of the order was shown wherever, by its original methods, it exerted itself to quiet disturbed communities. Wherever freedmen grew unruly, disguised horsemen appeared by night; and thereafter the darkies of the neighborhood inclined to stay under cover after daylight failed. But the order had grown too large, it was too widespread, the central authority was too remote from the local "dens," and the general scheme was too easily grasped and copied, to permit of the rigid exclusion from membership of such men as would incline to use violence, or to cover with the mantle of secrecy enterprises of a doubtful or even criminal cast. In Tennessee, the Brownlow government was bitterly hostile, and in September, 1868, the legislature passed a statute, aimed entirely at the Ku Klux, which went beyond the later congressional statutes in the penalties it prescribed for every act that could possibly imply complicity in the "conspiracy," and in the extraordinary powers conferred upon officers and all others who should aid in detecting or arresting Ku Klux. The members of the order were practically outlawed, and naturally felt bound in self-defense to resort to methods which the central officers could not approve. In

February, 1869, Governor Brownlow proclaimed martial law in several Tennessee counties, and the next day he ceased to be governor. The growing evils within the order, as well as the dangers which threatened it, doubtless made the wiser heads of the Klan readier to conclude that with the repeal of the alien and sedition laws and Brownlow's departure for the United States Senate its work in Tennessee was done. So, a few weeks later, by an order of the Grand Wizard, the Klan was formally disbanded, not only in Tennessee, but everywhere. It is generally understood that the Grand Wizard who issued that order was no less a person than Nathan Bedford Forrest. How many dens received the order at all, and how many of those that received it also obeyed it, will never be known, any more than it will be known how many dens there were, or how many members. However, the early spring of 1869 may be taken as the date when the Ku Klux Klan, which gave its name and its idea to the secret movement which began the undoing of reconstruction, ceased to exist as an organized body.

But the history of the original Ku Klux Klan is only a part—and perhaps not the most important part—of the movement which in the North was called the Ku Klux conspiracy, and which in the South is to this day regarded, with a truer sense of its historical importance, whatever one may think of the moral question, as comparable to that secret movement by which, under the very noses of French garrisons, Stein and Scharnhorst organized the great German struggle for liberty. Of the disguised bands which appeared and disappeared throughout the South so long as the carpet-baggers controlled the state governments, it is probable that not one half were veritable Ku Klux. Some were members of other orders, founded in imitation of the Ku Klux and using similar methods. Others were probably neighborhood affairs only. Yet others were simply bands of ruffians, operating in the night-time, and availing themselves of Ku Klux methods to attain personal ends which, whether criminal or not, were in no wise approved by the leaders in the Ku Klux and other similar organizations. How large a proportion of the violence and crime attributed to the Ku Klux should rightly be attributed to these lawless bands it is, of course, impossible to say; but it is certain that a number of those taken in disguise proved to be men of such antecedents, so clearly identified with the radical party, that they could not possibly have been members of the Ku Klux, the Knights of the White Camellia, or any other of the orders whose *raison d'être* was the revolt against radical rule.

The Knights of the White Camellia was probably the largest and most important of the orders—larger even than the true Ku Klux Klan. It was founded at New Orleans late in 1867 or early in 1868, and spread rapidly through the states lying east and west, from Texas to the Carolinas. A constitution adopted at New Orleans in June, 1868, provided for an elaborate organization by states, counties, and smaller communities, the affairs of the whole order being committed to a supreme council at New Orleans. The recollection of members, however, is to the effect that very little authority was really exercised by the supreme council or even by the state councils, that the county organizations were reasonably well maintained, and that in most respects each circle acted independently. The constitution and the oath and ceremonial of initiation commit the order to a very clear and decided position on the chief question of the day. Only white men, eighteen years of age or older, were admitted, and the initiate promised not merely to be secret and obedient, but "to maintain and defend the social and political superiority of the white race on this continent." The charge or lecture to the initiate set forth historical evidences of the superiority of the white race, made an argument for white supremacy, and painted the horrors of miscegenation. It enjoined fairness to negroes, and the concession to them of "the fullest measure of those rights which we recognize as theirs." The association, so the charge explained, was not a political party, and had no connection with any. The constitution, moreover, restricted the order from nominating or supporting candidates for office.

The "Pale Faces," the "Constitutional Union Guards," the "White Brotherhood," were other names borne by bands of men who did Ku Klux work. The majority of the congressional committee somehow got the idea that these were the real names, at different periods, of the one order which pervaded the entire South, and that "Ku Klux" was a name foisted upon the public, so that a member, when put upon the witness stand in a law court, might deny all knowledge of the organization. But the evidence of the existence of the true Ku Klux Klan, of its priority to all similar organizations of any importance, and of the existence of other orders with different names, is now too strong to permit of any doubt. The comparative strength of the various associations; the connection, if any there was, between them; their membership; the differences in their characters, aims, and methods—on these things it is not probable that any clear light will ever be thrown. Surviving members are themselves somewhat hazy on such questions. And indeed it is not of the first importance that they should be answered; for we have enough to show how the Ku Klux idea worked itself out, and with what results.

The working of the plan is exhibited more authoritatively than I could portray it in the memoranda of a gentle and kindly man, albeit a resolute wearer of a Confederate button, who, thirty years ago, was the absolute chief of the Knights of the White Camellia in a certain county in the heart of the Black Belt. Speaking of the county organization merely, he says:

The authority of the commander (this office I held) was *absolute*. All were sworn to obey his orders. There was an inner circle in each circle, to which was committed any particular work: its movements were not known to other members of the order. This was necessary, because, in our neighborhood, almost every Southern man was a member. At meetings of the full circle there was but little consideration as to work. The topic generally was law and order, and the necessity for organization. In fact, almost every meeting might have been public, so far as the discussions were concerned.

For the methods employed: in some cases they were severe, even extreme, but I believe they were necessary, although there was much wrong done when commanders were not the right men. There was too good an opportunity for individuals to take vengeance for personal grievances. A man, black or white, found dead in the road would furnish undisputed evidence that the Ku Klux Klan had been abroad. The officers of the law, even judges, were members; a jury could not be drawn without a majority of our men. In this county, no act of violence was committed by our circle. We operated on the terror inspired by the knowledge that we were organized. The carpet-baggers lived in constant dread of a visit, and were in great measure controlled through their fears. At one time, if one of our people threatened or abused a carpet-bagger, his house or stable would be fired that night.[1] . . . This occurred so often that it was impossible to separate the two events. Word was accordingly sent to a prominent carpet-bagger that if the thing happened again we would take him out at midday and hang him. There were no more fires.

The negroes had meetings at some point every night, obedience to the orders of the carpet-baggers, who kept them organized in this way. So long as their meetings were orderly we did not interfere; but when I got information that they were becoming disorderly and offensive, I ordered out a body of horsemen, who divided into squads, and stationed themselves where the negroes would pass on their way home. They were permitted to dress themselves in any fashion their fancies might dictate, but their orders were positive not to utter a word or molest a negro in any manner. I rarely had to send twice to the same neighborhood. Occasionally a large body was sent out to ride about all night with the same instructions as to silence. While the law against illegal voting had no penalty for the offense (no doubt an intentional omission) negroes often voted more than once at the same election. They assembled in such

---

[1] Here he refers to the oiling and firing of the stables of that particular Southern household in which the boyish inquiries I have referred to made a beginning of the investigations on which this paper is based.

crowds at the polls that one had almost to fight one's way to deposit a ballot. A body of our men was detailed on election day to go early and take possession, with the usual order for silence. Few negroes voted that day; none twice. No violence.

We put up with carpet-bag rule as long as we could stand it. Then a messenger was sent to each of them—they were filling all the county offices—to tell them we had decided they must leave. This was all that was needed. They had been expecting it, they said, and they left without making any resistance. Owing to some local circumstances, the circle at——was disbanded about the time of President Grant's proclamation, but we were not influenced by it in any degree. I think there were few cases of the disbandment of circles. The necessity for their existence expired with the exodus of the carpet-baggers.

That was the *modus operandi*, under a cautious and intelligent commander, in a neighborhood largely inhabited by men of birth and education. As it happens, the recollections of the commander are corroborated by one of the young men who obeyed his orders, now attorney general of the state, who adds that the proportion of "tomfoolery" to violence was about 1000 to 1. But even this straightforward recital of the successful performance of an apparently commendable work must make plain to any thoughtful reader the danger inseparable from the power of such an organization. In communities less intelligent, or where no such fit leader was chosen, the story was far different.

That violence was often used cannot be denied. Negroes were often whipped, and so were carpet-baggers. The incidents related in such stories as Tourgee's A Fool's Errand all have their counterparts in the testimony before congressional committees and courts of law. In some cases, after repeated warnings, men were dragged from their beds and slain by persons in disguise, and the courts were unable to find or to convict the murderers. Survivors of the orders affirm that such work was done, in most cases, by persons not connected with them or acting under their authority. It is impossible to prove or to disprove their statements. When such outrages were committed, not on worthless adventurers, who had no station in Northern communities from which they came, but on cultivated persons who had gone South from genuinely philanthropic motives—no matter how unwisely or tactlessly they went about their work—the effect was naturally to horrify and enrage the North.

The white teachers in the negro schools were probably the class which suffered most innocently, not ordinarily from violence, but from the countless other ways in which Southern society made them aware that they were unwelcome and that their mission was disapproved. They themselves, in too many instances, disregarded the boundary lines between different social classes, as rigid and cruel in democracies as anywhere else, and by associating themselves with freedmen made it unreasonable for them to expect any kindly recognition from men and women who, under other conditions, might have been their friends. They too often not merely disregarded, but even criticised and attacked, those usages and traditions which gave to Southern life a charm and distinction not elsewhere found in America. A wiser and more candid study of the conditions under which their work must be done, an avoidance of all hostility to whatever they might leave alone without sacrifice of principle, would perhaps have tempered the bitterness of Southern resentment at their presence. We may also admit that the sort of education they at first offered the freedmen was useless, or worse than useless—that theirs *was* a fool's errand. But they should never have been confounded with the creatures who came, not to help the negro, but to use him. The worst work the Ku Klux ever did was its opposition to negro schools, and the occasional expulsion or even violent handling of teachers. There were adventurers in the schoolhouses, and probably there were honest men in the legislatures, the courts, the executive offices; but as a class the teachers were far better than the others. The failure to discriminate in their favor doubtless did more than anything else to confirm the minds of honest and well-meaning people of the North in the belief that it was the baser elements of Southern society, and not its intelligent and responsible men, who had set to work to overthrow the carpet-bag régime.

The Ku Klux movement was not entirely underground. Sheeted horsemen riding about in the night-time were not its only forces. Secrecy and silence were indeed its main devices, but others were employed. The life of the carpet-bagger was made wretched otherwise than by dragging him from his bed and flogging him. The scorn in which he was held was made plain to him by averted faces or contemptuous glances on the street, by the obstacles he encountered in business, by the empty pews in his neighborhood when he went to church. If his children went to school, they were not asked to join in the play of other children, and must perforce fall back upon the companionship of little darkies. He himself, if he took the Southern view of "difficulties" and held himself ready to answer an insult with a blow, was sure to be accommodated whenever he felt belligerent. Probably not one in ten of his neighbors had given up the creed of the duello, though its ceremonial was not often observed. As for the "scalawag"—the Southerner who went over to the radicals—there was reserved for him a deeper hatred, a loftier contempt, than even the carpet-bagger got for his portion. No alien enemy, however despicable, is ever so loathed as a renegade.

But the Invisible Empire, however its sway was exercised, was everywhere a real empire. Wisely and humanely, or roughly and cruelly, the work was done. The state governments, under radical control, made little headway with their freedmen's militia against the silent representatives of the white man's will to rule. After 1870, even the blindest of the reconstruction leaders in Congress were made to see that they had built their house upon the sands. During the winter of 1870–71, Southern outrages were the subject of congressional debates and presidential messages.

In March, a Senate committee presented majority and minority reports on the result of its investigations in North Carolina. The majority found that there was an unjustifiable conspiracy, of a distinctly political nature, against the laws and against colored citizens. The minority found that the misgovernment and criminal exploiting of the Southern states by radical leaders had provoked a natural resistance and led to disorder and violence. In April, the first Ku Klux bill, "to enforce the Fourteenth Amendment," was passed; the President was empowered to use the troops, and even to suspend the writ of *habeas corpus*. In May, the second Ku Klux bill, "to enforce the right of citizens of the United States to vote," was passed. In October the President issued his proclamation. Troops were freely employed wherever there was an opportunity to use them, and the writ was suspended in nine counties of South Carolina. Hundreds of men were brought to trial before United States courts, under the two laws, and a number were convicted; but the leading men in the great orders were never reached. Northern writers have expressed the opinion that by the beginning of 1872 the "conspiracy" was overthrown. Nevertheless, the joint committee proceeded with its labors, and in February presented its great report on The Condition of Affairs in the Late Insurrectionary States. Majority and minority differed, as before; but the volume of reports and the twelve volumes of testimony enabled the minority to set forth with more convincing fullness the true nature of carpet-bag rule. In May, a bill extending the President's extraordinary powers over the next session of Congress passed the Senate, but was lost in the House. How much the action of Congress and the President had to do with the disappearance of the Ku Klux it is impossible to say. But after 1872 the Ku Klux did, for the most part, disappear; and so, in one state after another, did the carpet-bagger and the scalawag. The fox's skin had served its turn before it was cast aside.

Such, in brief outline, was the Ku Klux conspiracy according to the Northern view, the revolt against tyranny according to the Southern view, which was the beginning of the end of reconstruction. It was the unexpected outcome of a situation unexampled, and not even closely paralleled, in history. To many minds it seemed to nullify the war, the Emancipation Proclamation, and the constitutional amendments which were meant to seal forever the victory of the North over the South, and of liberty over slavery. To minds just as honest it seemed to reassert the great principles of the American Revolution. The majority of the congressional committee conducted their investigations after the manner of prosecuting attorneys dealing with ordinary criminals. The minority felt themselves bound to consider whether "an indictment against a whole people" would lie. To the majority "Ku Klux" meant simply outlaws; the minority thought that the first Ku Klux in history were the disguised men who, against the law, threw the tea overboard in Boston harbor.

The two views of the movement, like the movement itself and all that led up to it, are part and parcel of that division which was marked by Mason and Dixon's line. It was a division of institutions; it was a division of interests; it was and still is a division of character and habits of thought. Northern men had one idea of the strife, and Southern men an entirely different idea. The Southerners did not and could not regard themselves as rebels forced to be loyal. They knew they were beaten, and they gave up the fight; but they did not understand that they were bound to coöperate in any further plans of their conquerors. President Lincoln had made it plain that if the Union arms prevailed slavery must go, and the Southerners, in their state conventions of 1865, formally abolished it. Secession had been tried, and had failed as a policy; they declared that they would not try it again. Left for a moment to themselves, they set to work on an arrangement that would enable them to use under freedom the same sort of labor they had used under slavery, and made a place in the new order for the blacks, whom they could not reduce to slavery again, but whom they felt to be unfit for citizenship. Then Congress interfered and undid their work, and they stood passive until they could see what the congressional scheme would be like. They found it bad, oppressive, unwise, impossible. They bore it awhile in silence. Then in silence they made up their minds to resist. What form could their resistance take? It must be revolutionary, for they had formally renounced the right of secession. It could not be open war, for they were powerless to fight. So they made a secret revolution. Their rebellion could not raise its head, so it went underground.

If one asks of the movement, "Was it necessary?" this much, at least, may be answered: that no other plan of resistance would have served so well. If one asks, "Was it successful?" the answer is plain. No open revolt ever succeeded more completely. If one asks, "Was it justifiable?" the "yes" or "no" is harder to say. There must be much defining of terms, much patient separating of the accidental from the essential, much inquiry into motives. Describe the movement broadly as a secret movement, operating by terror and violence to nullify laws, and one readily condemns it. Paint all the conditions, enter into the minds and hearts of the men who lived under them, look at them through their eyes, suffer with their angry pain, and one revolts as their pride revolted. Weigh the broad rule, which is less a "light to guide" than a "rod to check," against the human impulse, and the balance trembles. One is ready to declare, not, perhaps, that the end justified the means, but that never before was an end so clearly worth fighting for made so clearly unattainable by any good means.

Nor does our hindsight much avail us. The end attained was mainly good. Southern society was righted. But the method of it survives in too many habits of the Southern mind, in too many shortcomings of Southern civilization, in too many characteristics of Southern life. The Southern whites, solidified in resistance to carpet-bag rule, have kept their solidarity unimpaired by any healthful division on public questions. Having learned a lesson, they cannot forget it. Seeing forms of law used to cloak oppression, and liberty invoked to countenance a tyranny, they learned to set men above political principles, and good government above freedom of thought. For thirty years they have continued to set one question above all others, and thus debarred themselves from full participation in the political life of the country. As they rule by fear, so by fear are they ruled. It is they themselves who are now befooled, and robbed of the nobler part of their own political birthright. They outdid their conquerors, yet they are not free.

Washington During Reconstruction

S. W. McCALL

Washington during reconstruction was a reflection of the country, as is always likely to be the case when there is a great opinion pending upon which public attention is fixed. Doubtless a complexity of problems may sometimes occur, when a majority of the people are willing to accept something they do not want in order to secure something they want badly. And it is never quite safe to point confidently to a popular verdict, upon a minor issue of a campaign, in which some overshadowing issue was pending. But there was little contradiction of issues in the North during and immediately after the war, and the North at that time absolutely wielded the political power of the nation. Everything else was lost sight of in the effort, first to save the Union, then to secure freedom, and after these objects had been attained, to establish such a basis of restoration as should effectively guard them both from future danger. The sentiment of the Northern people was fixed beyond change upon the supreme necessity of maintaining freedom and the Union, and there was little danger that upon those questions their representatives would prove unresponsive to their will.

One of the first tasks confronting the statesmen at Washington who dealt with the problem of reconstruction consisted in clearing away the metaphysics with which it was surrounded. The purely theoretical phases of the situation continued for nearly five years. The tendency of masses of men to divide on abstractions, and to become confused by them, was well illustrated in the progress of reconstruction. Whether the Southern states had really been in or out of the Union during the war; whether they were "dead states," or their "practical relations" to the Union only had been disturbed, were questions of little more practical consequence than some of the distinctions in theology, and yet these were the features of reconstruction which were chiefly discussed until the conclusion of the war. The vital point in the situation was that there had actually been four years of bloody war, in which several hundreds of thousands of lives and some billions of dollars of property had been destroyed. Doubtless an important part of the work of reconstruction consisted in the restoration of the blessings of civil government to the localities which had so long been the theatre of war, but a far more important part was involved in the performance of an obvious duty, alike due to the conquerors and the conquered. How should the nation be protected against a repetition of so terrible a struggle? How should the good results of the war be made permanent? For it would certainly have been criminal folly if those responsible for the conduct of the government had, on account of any fine-spun theory about the legal effect of attempted secession upon the status of the Southern states, neglected to exact the utmost security for the future.

The use of so mild a term as "insurrection" did not change the character of the struggle, which had been, as a matter of fact, one of the bloodiest and most expensive of wars, from which the nation was fortunate to escape with its life. The Southern states had yielded to no sheriff's posse, but to an army of two millions of men; and it would have been very little to the credit of the statesmen at Washington if they had permitted the tremendous fact of war to be obscured by some legal phrase, and had devised remedies for the phrase, and not for the exact situation. When the time came for the final solution of the question, theory yielded to fact, and it was treated as a question of grave practical statesmanship, having peculiar and difficult conditions of its own, rather than one to be settled by technical distinctions. The wisdom of the men at Washington who dealt with the problem was, very likely, not so luminous and perfect as that which gentlemen now possesses upon the same subject, a generation afterward; but such wisdom as they had they finally employed with reference to the actual situation, and for the primary purpose of securing to the whole nation whatever good results had sprung out of the war, and of delivering it from the danger of another struggle on account of the same cause. There may be room to question the wisdom of the remedies they devised, but there can be none that they took the proper point of view.

There existed, however, a class of difficulties of a constitutional character, which increased the magnitude of the work. The restoration of the supremacy of civil law, after the suppression of a rebellion against a government such as exists in England, would present a much simpler problem. That government would deal directly with individuals, and with them alone; it would not come in contact with subordinate jurisdictions; and, as the disturbed areas should become pacified, the military character of the rule would by degrees become mitigated by the gradual restoration of civil rights, until finally the peaceful sway of the laws should be restored. The federal character of our government, as well as the fact that it derived all its vitality through the limited provisions of a written constitution, made our problem a complex one. When the Southern states should be restored to the Union, or if they had never been out of the Union, then when they should again be permitted to participate in the common government, they would resume their equality with the other states and the control of a wide range of governmental powers, free from the supervision of the central government. The mere restoration of courts, sheriffs, and other agencies of civil government was what the task presented, in common with the task of restoration after rebellion against governments simple and unlimited in character. But, in addition to that, it was necessary to provide against results likely to follow the setting in motion of local sovereignties whose powers would be no less firmly secured to them by the Constitution than those of the national government itself. It thus became necessary to provide securities for the future, constitutional in character, and applicable alike to the states which fought for as well as to those which fought against the Union.

The situation was not lacking in other elements of difficulty. The resistance to the national authority had extended over the vast region stretching from the Potomac to the Rio Grande, and containing three quarters of a million square miles of territory. Over this enormous area, greater in extent than Italy, Spain, France, and the German Empire combined, there were scattered four millions of black men, who had been held as slaves and had been made free. If they had been freed by the ordinary peaceful agencies, operating in the territory where slavery existed, the forces which secured their freedom might have been relied upon to protect it; but they had been forcibly emancipated by external agencies. Their masters had not given them up because they desired to do so, but because they had been compelled by overwhelming force; and before the withdrawal of the military arm, and the reestablishment of state government with their great power over individual liberty, the most careful measures were required to secure the freedom which was the most important outcome of the war.

I have referred to some of the salient difficulties which obviously could not have been fully developed until the end of the war, and I will now refer to the principal features of legislation, from which it will appear that there was a constant evolution toward a more radical treatment of the subject. Hostilities had scarcely begun before a discussion was entered upon in Congress which involved the principles on which reconstruction should proceed. At the famous special session, called soon after the opening of the war, both houses of Congress passed the so-called Crittenden Resolutions by nearly a unanimous vote. These resolutions did not embody a basis of reconstruction, but they promulgated principles which would have profoundly affected that process if they had been applied. They declared that the war was not waged for the purpose of conquest or to overthrow the institutions of any state, but to maintain the Constitution and Union "with all the dignity, equality, and rights of the several states unimpaired." A few men of the more radical wing of the Republican party, among whom were Sumner, Lovejoy, and Stevens, refused to vote for these resolutions. "Ask them who made the war," said Stevens, "what is its object." Under these resolutions, put forth with such an approach to unanimity, reconstruction would have been an extremely simple process. In fact, it would have been automatic, and it would have rested with any of the seceding states to determine when it should stop fighting and exercise its rights under the Constitution, and among them the right of representation in Congress. Sentiment, however, developed rapidly; and when, at the beginning of the following session, an attempt was made to reaffirm the same resolutions, they were, upon the motion of Stevens, laid upon the table by a decisive vote of the very House which, but a few months before, had passed them so strongly.

Lincoln's practical attempt at reconstruction, embodied in the "Louisiana plan," was as summarily dealt with by Congress as the Crittenden Resolutions had been. Lincoln, however, at the time he put forth this plan, did not enjoy the prestige which he subsequently gained. It is hardly conceivable that Congress would have dared, even one year afterward, to accord such contemptuous treatment to any important policy which he might have proposed. The terms of the Louisiana proclamation permitted the greater number of those who had borne arms against the government to take part in the work of reconstruction, upon taking an oath to support the Constitution and the laws relating to slavery. The congressional opposition was directed against the liberality of this plan, and especially to the feature of it which accorded recognition to a state if so small a number as one tenth of its voters should comply with the terms of the proclamation. Mr. Henry Winter Davis, of Maryland, was especially hostile, and led the opposition to the policy of the President with conspicuous ability. Lincoln's policy was set aside, and a bill, advocated by Davis, was passed by both houses of Congress.

There was one serious objection to the plan proposed by Lincoln. He treated reconstruction as an executive act, and it was possible that the states complying with the terms of his proclamation might be recognized by the executive department, and at the same time that the two houses of Congress might refuse admission to the members whom the states might choose. A state might thus be reconstructed and again in the Union so far as the Executive was concerned, and unreconstructed and out of the Union so far as the most important function of representation in Congress was concerned. In this very instance, the states which complied with Lincoln's proclamation were denied representation in Congress. The question of reconstruction thus became still more complicated at the outset, and the foundation was laid for the struggle between the executive and the legislative department which culminated in the impeachment of Johnson. Obviously the process of restoring a state to its practical relations with the Union required the concurrence of both the legislative and the executive department. If the plan so eloquently advocated by Davis, and substituted by Congress for that of the President, had been accepted by Lincoln, the work of reconstruction would probably have been accomplished upon more stringent lines, indeed, than he proposed, but upon lines which were vastly more liberal than those finally adopted. Lincoln, however, by permitting Congress to adjourn without signing the bill of the congressional leaders, practically vetoed it, and nothing was accomplished by this effort in the solution of the question.

Mr. Thaddeus Stevens had logically taken the position, from the very outbreak of hostilities, that a condition of war existed, within the meaning of that term in the law of nations; that the Southern states had forfeited all their rights under the Constitution; and that after they had been conquered they should be dealt with practically as conquered territory, without any constitutional rights. This was regarded as an extreme doctrine; but in spite of the fact that he found, when he first advocated it, only the slightest support, he adhered to it with remarkable consistency, and in the end it was the theory which found practical acceptance. The constitutional theory involved in this plan was not less simple than that contained in the Crittenden Resolutions, although at the opposite extreme. This was really the important point upon which the so-called radicalism of Stevens was influential. It consisted in adopting the very matter-of-fact policy of doing what the future continuance of the national life, which had been saved by so many sacrifices, demanded, and treating reconstruction as a practical rather than a theoretical question. It obviously did not involve negro suffrage. That might or might not be one of the "terms" which should be imposed. Stevens did not originate the idea of imposing negro suffrage as a necessary part of reconstruction, and the opinion entertained in some quarters that he was especially responsible for the introduction of that idea is widely at variance with the facts. His first plan was embodied in an amendment to the Constitution, basing representation upon the number of voters in the different states, and thus making it for the political interest of the states to establish a broad suffrage in order to increase their representation in Congress; and so late as the 30th of April, 1866, he reported to the House the Fourteenth Amendment in the form in which it now stands in the Constitution, and at the same time a bill declaring that when that amendment should have been incorporated in the Constitution, and any state "lately in insurrection" should have ratified it and adopted a constitution and laws in accordance with its terms, it should be admitted to representation in Congress. That policy lacked neither simplicity nor moderation. In the December preceding, Sumner had presented to the Senate a resolution demanding "the complete enfranchisement of all citizens, so that there shall be no denial of rights on account of race or color." Lincoln had suggested the suffrage for the freedmen, but on the condition that it should be conferred gradually and as they should become fitted for it—a condition full of wise policy for the country at large, and of humanity for the negro. But whoever may have been its advocates, negro suffrage resulted from the course of events rather than from the efforts of any individuals.

Lincoln, just before his death, had prepared a new plan of reconstruction, and there can be little doubt that he would soon have promulgated it if his life had been spared. On his accession to the presidency Johnson accepted Lincoln's cabinet in its entirety, and he also finally accepted the latter's plan of reconstruction, although his first utterances had alarmed even the radicals by the hostility of his tone toward the South. This plan, which may fairly be called Lincoln's second plan, was more severe than that embodied in the Louisiana proclamation, but it repeated the fatal error of treating reconstruction as a function of the Executive. If Lincoln had lived, his great political influence might have been sufficient to secure the adoption of this programme by Congress; but whether Congress had accepted it or not, he would doubtless have had sufficient sagacity not to become involved in the bitter controversy to which Johnson became a party. After the latter, however, had accepted the plan which he received, already prepared, at the hands of Lincoln's cabinet, he adhered to it uncompromisingly and with very little discretion.

A potent force in overturning this plan was found in the result of its own workings. It had an opportunity to be tested. It was promulgated during a long recess of Congress, and its operation was entered upon free from legislative interference. Before Congress had reassembled it had been put in force in nearly all the Southern states. They had chosen legislatures, had elected Representatives and Senators in Congress, passed local laws, and set up the machinery of government under the protection of the national military forces. Congress was called upon to deal not simply with a proposition for a policy, but with a scheme, already put in execution, which was working somewhat badly. The first attempts at legislation on the part of the new governments were ill advised, to say the least, and were directed to the great question upon which the conscience of the North was thoroughly aroused—the preservation of the freedom of the negro. The counter revolution, also, seemed to be moving somewhat too rapidly for the Northern people. Its motion may be well illustrated by a single circumstance, by no means exceptional in character. When the session of Congress ended, on the 3d of March, 1865, military operations were being conducted on a broad scale, and Mr. Alexander H. Stephens was Vice President of the Southern Confederacy. When Congress came together at its next session, the credentials of Stephens were presented as Senator elect from Georgia; and as if this were not sufficiently startling, there were urged on his behalf constitutional reasons why he should be permitted to take the oath of office. Stephens might have made a very acceptable Senator, but the men composing the Republican majority in Congress would have been something less, or more, than human, if, at that time, while the fire of battle was still hot, they could have regarded this spectacle with entire complacency.

The decisive influence, however, which brought about the destruction of the President's plan grew out of the anti-negro laws, which were passed by nearly all of the legislatures chosen in pursuance of it. A bare survey of those laws will convince one of their utter lack of policy, as well as of their gross injustice, and they find no palliation in the poor excuse that has been made for them: that laws with somewhat similar features, relating to apprentices and tramps, may be found upon the statute books of some of the Northern states. There is at the outset the material point of difference that the "tramp" and "apprentice" laws referred to applied impartially to all races. The few Northern statutes, too, were scattered over a great many years; they were proportionately less severe in character, and some of them followed reconstruction in point of time. But if they were similar in principle and had preceded reconstruction, still it would surely have been a strange exhibition of political wisdom on the part of the Southern legislatures to extract these scattered precedents and condense the application of them in their very first legislative acts, when the North was anxiously observing how the freedom which had been so expensively purchased should be regarded by the Southern people. Some of those laws established a condition not greatly different from the former slavery, and in some respects it differed for the worse.

A condition of public sentiment was soon produced where the solution of the problem of reconstruction that was ultimately reached became inevitable. In the piping times of peace, statesmen may patch up difficulties without much reference to public opinion, for the simple reason that the public is often not aroused upon them, and cares very little how they may be solved; but it is pretty safe to take for granted that great masses of men, of the same race, will, under similar conditions, take the same action on any great question concerning which they are profoundly stirred. The action of the Southern legislatures was very likely entirely natural, under the circumstances; but it reacted strongly upon the Northern people, and produced a course of action on their part which was also entirely natural. It is a very simple method of treatment to portray the leaders on one side as absolutely judicious and free from fault, and those on the other as malign demagogues, acting under the influence of pure hatred and malevolence. But the course of reconstruction must be accounted for upon broad principles of human nature. It was not a haphazard affair, but sprung inevitably out of the war, the fervent passion for human liberty which appeared again to be in danger, the wrought-up patriotism, and the kindled fury of partisanship in the clashing of the great departments of the government. The men who especially voiced the popular sentiment in Congress were indeed the fit and natural leaders; but if they had retired to private life at the end of the war, events would have compelled substantially the same results under new leaders. They would have been impotent to control, even if they had resisted, the popular forces which were pushing them onward.

The working of Johnson's plan inevitably destined it to defeat, but how harsh a measure would its failure make necessary? The first proposal certainly was not a radical one. As has been seen, nearly a year after Johnson put forth his proclamation, Stevens reported to the House the Fourteenth Amendment to the Constitution, together with the bill basing reconstruction upon its acceptance. Before this bill was acted upon by Congress that amendment had been submitted to the states, and every Southern state had contemptuously refused to accept it. What should the statesmen at Washington do? Propose a plan which had been rejected in advance? In the meantime, the question had been carried before the people at an election, and the result was to strengthen enormously the hands of the opponents of the President's policy. A decided impulse was given to the idea that liberty should not be risked by a continuance of such a course of legislation as the first efforts of the Southern legislatures had produced, but that it should be armed with the ballot for its own protection. At the ensuing session of Congress, the policy of complete enfranchisement, without regard to color, which Sumner had put forth in his resolutions of the preceding year, and had supported in one of the most elaborate speeches of even his career, was adopted as a basis of reconstruction. Sumner had advocated the ballot "as a peacemaker, a schoolmaster, a protector." Undoubtedly the Northern public had come to regard it especially necessary as a "protector," and the final reconstruction act was passed, overturning the Johnson governments, and substituting for them a drastic system of military government, to continue until the new conditions of reconstruction were complied with, and coupling with it a provision for the extension of suffrage to the emancipated blacks. The control of some of the Southern states was thus put in the hands of electors, a majority of whom possessed no education, and had never had the slightest experience in self-government. Among the earliest results of the franchise thus suddenly imposed, public treasuries were robbed, courts paralyzed, property extinguished; and a point was soon reached where it became apparent that the equality established at the ballot box could be maintained only at the price of civilization.

The plan of reconstruction, therefore, was one for which there was a divided responsibility. One event logically followed another, and the people of one section, no less than those of the other, are entitled to credit or blame for what occurred. The Southern people, who had yielded to superior force, but whose hearts were still unsubdued, cannot be reproached for taking that course which was entirely natural, and indeed inevitable, in the conditions that then existed. But, on the other hand, invective should stop short of denouncing another people—those who had won victory at such a tremendous cost, and who had presented to their view evidence of a clearly defined danger to the freedom which had been gained.

Johnson himself is not to be ignored as a factor in bringing about the result. He cannot be criticised for adopting the plan of Lincoln, but he executed it in a manner that encouraged the Southern people to believe that they had gained to their side, at the threshold of the solution of the war problems, the great powers of the presidency. Undoubtedly there is no room to question his patriotism, which was conspicuous during the war, and no less so when he resisted the encroachments of Congress upon the powers of his office. But if he had possessed something of the spirit of compromise; something, also, of the political sagacity and the ability to control men that appeared in such large measure in the character of Lincoln, there would certainly have been no collision between the two great departments of the government, and probably reconstruction would have proceeded on the basis which involved the acceptance of the muniments against slavery, and of the great provisions of the Fourteenth Amendment. It would then have rested with the Southern states to decide whether those measures should be accepted, or harsher ones applied; and, without the encouragement of executive support, they would probably have accepted the terms which they had declined under the conditions existing when they were offered.

But Johnson's characteristics were such as to augment rather than to diminish the difference between Congress and himself. He can never be magnified into a great statesman. He was narrow and obstinate, and he made himself all but impossible as a leader, on account of his singular lack of decorum in speech; but he was honest and unswerving in his adherence to certain great principles of government, and he defended them with a courage which inspires respect for his character. Congress, on its side, proved sufficiently obstinate, and, since the President would not surrender, the two-thirds majority in both houses, which made the veto of no consequence, was used to strip him of the great powers of his office. Because he would not yield to this encroachment; because he adhered to the constitutional construction of those powers which had prevailed since the foundation of the government, and which, after his brief term in the presidency, was again recurred to, the leaders of the House saw fit to impeach him. They had been rapidly reducing to a mere governmental figurehead the great constitutional office of the presidency, with its powers as clearly defined as were those of Congress itself, and which existed, not for the man who held the office, but in trust for the whole people.

A review of the impeachment proceedings is not within the scope of this article, but they will be referred to, to illustrate the intense feeling which had been engendered between the President and Congress by the struggle over reconstruction, and also to call to mind the personality of those especially concerned in the development of the national policy toward the Southern states. The President, on his part, had acted up to the old Jacksonian models, and made an unsparing use of the federal offices to reward the friends and to punish the enemies of his policy. If he had confined himself to the obstinately maintained lines on which he had battled for his plan of reconstruction, he would doubtless have had his veto overridden, and would have been the constant mark of highly wrought and hostile declamation, but he would probably have escaped impeachment; but when he struck at the offices, he dealt a blow at what was then, as it has always been, a sore spot in the make-up of the average Congressman. A violation of the Constitution is a somewhat general and indefinite crime, the consequences of which do not especially come home to the ordinary member; but when his district or state is invaded, and his friends are ruthlessly turned out of post offices and clerkships and custom houses, and his enemies put in their places, freedom is very apt to shriek.

Congress responded to the President by the Tenure of Office

Act, which put him very securely under the safe guardianship of the Senate in making removals from office. The holders of executive offices thus became responsible, in the last resort, to the Senate, and not to the President, who was the constitutional agent of the people in the execution of the laws. The policy of the new theory was forcibly illustrated in the case of Stanton, who was discharging the important duties of the office of Secretary of War without consultation with his executive chief, and who would occasionally send a message to Congress. Of course, very little would be left of the great office of the presidency under such a system, and whether from purely patriotic motives or a regard for his own personal importance, in which he was not entirely lacking, Johnson refused tamely to submit. He made short work of removing Stanton; and when the Senate declined to concur, under the Office Act, he treated that piece of legislation as a constitutional nullity, and defiantly removed him again. Stanton represented in his person every postmaster and other federal officeholder in the country who had been confirmed by the Senate. By this act Johnson invited impeachment, and under the tremendous political excitement prevailing at that time, not only in Washington, but throughout the North, over the great measures connected with reconstruction, the invitation was certain of acceptance. The wonder is that, in a Senate of which not one sixth of the members had been elected as Democrats, enough Republican Senators should be found, in a proceeding saturated with partisan spirit, to vote against the position of that party, and acquit the President. For when the final vote was taken, the judicial and legal weight of the party was found on the side of Johnson.

I have said the impeachment well illustrated the partisan rancor growing out of reconstruction, and also the personality of the important actors in the reconstruction drama. Johnson was of course the central figure, both in the trial and in the attempts which were made to restore the Southern states to their former standing in the Union. Stanton's removal was the immediate occasion of the impeachment; and strangely enough, Stanton had been an advocate, and was probably even one of the authors, of the President's plan of reconstruction. He was a great secretary, and he possessed in a high degree, also, the qualities of obstinacy and imperiousness which distinguished Johnson. Stevens, aptly termed by Mr. Dawes "a great intellectual gladiator," represented more strongly than any other man the position of Congress upon the question of reconstruction, and he it was who was fittingly chosen to arraign the President at the bar of the Senate. The cause of the House lost much on account of his inability to take a more prominent part in the trial; for, in a long and stormy public and professional career, he had never come in conflict with his intellectual superior. To Boutwell, who had been chosen as the leading manager, and who, with remarkable self-sacrifice, had refused to accept it, in order to secure full harmony among the managers, must be given the credit of having contributed more by his industry and judicious management toward making the cause of the House successful than any of his colleagues. He also was a conspicuous supporter of the congressional plan of reconstruction. Charles Sumner, the most ornate if not the greatest orator of the Senate, was one of the original advocates of negro suffrage, and he was a bitter and unsparing enemy of Johnson, both in his policy and at his trial. His passionate opinion, filed in the case, in the extreme character of its views upon the proceeding as well as upon the scope of the process of impeachment, is likely to remain one of the curiosities of the trial.

Fessenden, who was shrewd, cautious, statesmanlike, a great debater, an ardent Republican, and yet hostile to the impeachment, probably deserves to be regarded as the greatest Senator of the war period. His course during the trial was most influential. He was also the chairman, on the part of the Senate, of the committee on reconstruction, and signed, with Stevens, the celebrated report, which it is impossible to read and escape the conclusion that the President's policy of reconstruction was unwise. Trumbull was another strongly partisan Republican, but to his judicial temperament, and to the fact that he was the greatest lawyer in the Senate, it is doubtless due that he opposed the impeachment. He was also uncompromising in his hostility to the President's policy of reconstruction. Evarts, who managed the President's defense with such consummate ability, was the most successful trial lawyer of his time, and only escaped being a great orator by an involved method of statement and a diffuseness of style. His influence afterward, as Johnson's Attorney General, undoubtedly contributed to a suspension of the warfare between Congress and the President. Curtis, who was the principal associate of Evarts in the defense of the President, was not identified with either the legislation or the administration of laws relating to reconstruction. His contribution to the trial was memorable, and very little ground for convicting the President survived the coldly legal argument, running through two days, with which he hopelessly shattered the case of the managers.

Undoubtedly some great evils resulted from the plan of reconstruction that was ultimately adopted, but it by no means follows that any other plan would have worked with absolute smoothness and with no injurious results. However common wisdom after the fact may be, it is not always safe to indulge in it. Looking at the course of events that developed under the brief application of Johnson's policy, it is apparent that if reconstruction had gone on to the end under that policy, the historian would have had other evils to portray, compared with which the looting of Southern treasuries might be mild indeed. Under the plan that was finally put in execution we have at least secured peace and freedom, and have witnessed a remarkable improvement in the condition of the negro race. That is indeed much—as much as in a broad view could fairly have been looked for. The statesmen at Washington were not dealing with ideal conditions. Centuries of slavery could not be uprooted in a day without leaving enormous social problems to be solved. And care must be taken not to attribute to the working of legislation those penalties which society must inevitably pay for a long persistence in evil courses.

The Undoing of Reconstruction

WILLIAM A. DUNNING

In July of 1870, when the law declaring Georgia entitled to representation in Congress was finally enacted, the process of reconstruction was, from the technical point of view, complete. Each of the states which had seceded from the Union had been "made over" by the creation of a new political people, in which the freedmen constituted an important element, and the organization of a new government, in the working of which the participation of the blacks on equal terms with the whites was put under substantial guarantees. The leading motive of the Reconstruction had been, at the inception of the process, to insure to the freedmen an effective protection of their civil rights—of life, liberty, and property. In the course of the process, the chief stress came to be laid on the endowment of the blacks with full political rights—with the electoral franchise and eligibility to office. And by the time the process was complete, a very important, if not the most important part had been played by the desire and the purpose to secure to the Republican party the permanent control of several Southern states in which hitherto

134

such a political organization had been unknown. This last motive had a plausible and widely accepted justification in the view that the rights of the negro and the "results of the war" in general would be secure only if the national government should remain indefinitely in Republican hands, and that therefore the strengthening of the party was a primary dictate of patriotism.

Through the operation of these various motives, successive and simultaneous, the completion of the Reconstruction showed the following situation: (1) the negroes were in the enjoyment of equal political rights with the whites; (2) the Republican party was in vigorous life in all the Southern states, and in firm control of many of them; and (3) the negroes exercised an influence in political affairs out of all relation to their intelligence or property, and, since so many of the whites were disfranchised, excessive even in proportion to their numbers. At the present day, in the same states, the negroes enjoy practically no political rights; the Republican party is but the shadow of a name; and the influence of the negroes in political affairs is nil. This contrast suggests what has been involved in the undoing of Reconstruction.

Before the last state was restored to the Union the process was well under way through which the resumption of control by the whites was to be effected. The tendency in this direction was greatly promoted by conditions within the Republican party itself. Two years of supremacy in those states which had been restored in 1868 had revealed unmistakable evidences of moral and political weakness in the governments. The personnel of the party was declining in character through the return to the North of the more substantial of the carpet-baggers, who found Southern conditions, both social and industrial, far from what they had anticipated, and through the very frequent instances in which the "scalawags" ran to open disgrace. Along with this deterioration in the white element of the party, the negroes who rose to prominence and leadership were very frequently of a type which acquired and practiced the tricks and knavery rather than the useful arts of politics, and the vicious courses of these negroes strongly confirmed the prejudices of the whites. But at the same time that the incapacity of the party in power to administer any government was becoming demonstrable, the problems with which it was required to cope were made by its adversaries such as would have taxed the capacity of the most efficient statesmen the world could produce. Between 1868 and 1870, when the cessation of the national military authority left the new state governments to stand by their own strength, there developed that widespread series of disorders with which the name of the Ku Klux is associated. While these were at their height the Republican party was ousted from control in five of the old rebel states—Tennessee, North Carolina, Texas, Georgia, and Virginia. The inference was at once drawn that the whites of the South were pursuing a deliberate policy of overthrowing the negro party by violence. No attention was paid to the claim that the manifest inefficiency and viciousness of the Republican governments afforded a partial, if not a wholly adequate explanation of their overthrow. Not even the relative quiet and order that followed the triumph of the whites in these states were recognized as justifying the new régime. The North was deeply moved by what is considered evidence of a new attack on its cherished ideals of liberty and equality, and when the Fifteenth Amendment had become part of the Constitution, Congress passed the Enforcement Acts and the laws for the federal control of elections. To the forces making for the resumption of white government in the South was thus opposed that same apparently irresistible power which had originally overthrown it.

That the Ku Klux movement was to some extent the expression of a purpose not to submit to the political domination of the blacks is doubtless true. But many other motives were at work in the disorders, and the purely political antithesis of the races was not so clear in the origin and development of the movement as in connection with the efforts of the state governments to suppress it. Thousands of respectable whites, who viewed the Ku Klux outrages with horror, turned with equal horror from the projects of the governments to quell the disturbances by a negro militia. Here was the crux of the race issue. Respectable whites would not serve with the blacks in the militia; the Republican state governments would not—and indeed, from the very nature of the case, could not—exclude the blacks from the military service; the mere suggestion of employing the blacks alone in such service turned every white into practically a sympathizer with the Ku Klux: and thus the government was paralyzed at the foundation of its authority. It was demonstrated again and again that the appearance of a body of negroes under arms, whether authorized by law or not, had for its most certain result an affray, if not a pitched battle, with armed whites, in which the negroes almost invariably got the worst of it.

On the assumption, then, that the white state governments in the South were unwilling, and the black governments were unable, to protect the negro in his rights, Congress inaugurated the policy of the "Force Acts." The primary aim was to protect the right to vote, but ultimately the purely civil rights, and even the so-called "social rights," were included in the legislation. By the act of 1870, a long series of minutely specified offenses, involving violence, intimidation, and fraud, with the effect or even the intention of denying equal rights to any citizens of the United States, were made crimes and misdemeanors, and were thus brought under the jurisdiction of the federal courts. Great activity was at once displayed by the United States district attorneys throughout the South, and hundreds of indictments were brought in; but convictions were few. The whites opposed to the process of the federal courts, supported by federal troops, no such undisguised resistance as had often been employed against state officers backed by a posse comitatus or a militia company of negroes. But every advantage was taken of legal technicalities; in the regions where the Ku Klux were strong, juries and witnesses were almost invariably influenced by sympathy or terror to favor the accused; and the huge disproportion between the number of arrests and the number of convictions was skillfully employed to sustain the claim that the federal officers were using the law as the cover for a systematic intimidation and oppression of the whites. As the effect of this first act seemed to be rather an increase than a decrease in the disorders of the South, Congress passed in the following year a more drastic law. This, known commonly as the Ku Klux Act, healed many technical defects in the earlier law; reformulated in most precise and far-reaching terms the conspiracy clause, which was especially designed to cover Ku Klux methods; and, finally, authorized the President, for a limited time, to suspend the writ of habeas corpus, and employ military force in the suppression of violence and crime in any given district. In addition to the punitive system thus established, Congress at the same time instituted a rigorous preventive system through the Federal Elections Laws. By acts of 1871 and 1872, every polling place, in any election for Congressmen, might be manned by officials appointed by the federal courts, with extensive powers for the detection of fraud, and with authority to employ the federal troops in the repression of violence.

Through the vigorous policy thus instituted by the national government the movement toward the resumption of control by the whites in the South met with a marked though temporary check. The number of convictions obtained under the Ku Klux Act was not large, and President Grant resorted in but a single instance—that of certain counties in South Carolina, in the autumn of 1871—to the extraordinary powers conferred upon him. But the moral effect of what was done was very great, and the evidence that the whole power of the national government could and would be exerted on the side of the blacks produced a salutary change in method among the whites. The extreme and

violent element was reduced to quiescence, and haste was made
more slowly. No additional state was redeemed by the whites
until 1874. Meanwhile, the wholesale removal of political disabilities by Congress in 1872 brought many of the old and respected Southern politicians again into public life, with a corresponding improvement in the quality of Democratic leadership. More deference began to be paid to the Northern sentiment
hostile to the Grant administration which had been revealed in
the presidential campaign of 1872, and the policy of the Southern
whites was directed especially so as to bring odium upon the use
of the military forces in the states yet to be wrested from black
control.

It was upon the support of the federal troops that the whole
existence of the remaining black governments in the South came
gradually to depend. Between 1872 and 1876 the Republican
party split in each of the states in which it still retained control,
and the fusion of one faction with the Democrats gave rise to
disputed elections, general disorder, and appeals by the radical
Republicans to the President for aid in suppressing domestic violence. Alabama and Arkansas emerged from the turmoil in 1874
with the whites triumphant; and the federal troops, after per-
forming useful service in keeping the factions from serious
bloodshed, ceased to figure in politics. But in Louisiana and
South Carolina the radical factions retained power exclusively
through the presence of the troops, who were employed in the
former state to reconstitute both the legislature and the executive at the bidding of one of the claimants of the gubernatorial
office. The very extraordinary proceedings in New Orleans
greatly emphasized the unfavorable feeling at the North toward
"governments resting on bayonets"; and when, upon the approach of the state election of 1875 in Mississippi, the radical
governor applied for troops to preserve order, President Grant
rather tartly refused to furnish them. The result was the overthrow of black government in that state. Though strenuously

denied at the time, it was no deep secret that the great negro majority in the state was overcome in this campaign by a quiet but general exertion of every possible form of pressure to keep the blacks from the polls. The extravagance and corruption of the state administration had become so intolerable to the whites that questionable means of terminating it were admitted by even the most honorable without question. There was relatively little "Ku-Kluxing" or open violence, but in countless ways the negroes were impressed with the idea that there would be peril for them in voting. "Intimidation" was the word that had vogue at the time, in describing such methods, and intimidation was illegal. But if a party of white men, with ropes conspicuous on their saddlebows, rode up to a polling place and announced that hanging would begin in fifteen minutes, though without any more definite reference to anybody, and a group of blacks who had assembled to vote heard the remark and promptly disappeared, votes were lost, but a conviction on a charge of intimidation was difficult. Or if an untraceable rumor that trouble was impending over the blacks was followed by the mysterious appearance of bodies of horsemen on the roads at midnight, firing guns and yelling at nobody in particular, votes again were lost, but no crime or misdemeanor could be brought home to any one. Devices like these were familiar in the South, but on this occasion they were accompanied by many other evidences of a purpose on the part of the whites to carry their point at all hazards. The negroes, though numerically much in excess of the whites, were very definitely demoralized by the aggressiveness and unanimity of the latter, and in the ultimate test of race strength the weaker gave way.

The "Mississippi plan" was enthusiastically applied in the remaining three states, Louisiana, South Carolina, and Florida, in the elections of 1876. Here, however, the presence of the federal troops and of all the paraphernalia of the Federal Elections Laws materially stiffened the courage of the negroes, and the result of the state election became closely involved in the controversy over the presidential count. The Southern Democratic leaders fully appreciated the opportunity of their position in this controversy, and, through one of those bargains without words which are common in great crises, the inauguration of President Hayes was followed by the withdrawal of the troops from the support of the last radical governments, and the peaceful lapse of the whole South into the control of the whites.

With these events of 1877 the first period in the undoing of reconstruction came to an end. The second period, lasting till 1890, presented conditions so different from the first as entirely to transform the methods by which the process was continued. Two, indeed, of the three elements which have been mentioned as summing up reconstruction still characterized the situation: the negroes were precisely equal in rights with the other race, and the Republican party was a powerful organization in the South. As to the third element, the disproportionate political influence of the blacks, a change had been effected, and their power had been so reduced as to correspond much more closely to their general social significance. In the movement against the still enduring features of reconstruction the control of the state governments by the whites was of course a new condition of the utmost importance, but not less vital was the party complexion of the national government. From 1875 to 1889 neither of the great parties was at any one time in effective control of both the presidency and the two houses of Congress. As a consequence, no partisan legislation could be enacted. Though the state of affairs in the South was for years a party issue of the first magnitude, the legislative deadlock had for its general result a policy of non-interference by the national government, and the whites were left to work out in their own way the ends they had in view. Some time was necessary, however, to overcome the influence of the two bodies of legislation already on the national statute book—the Force Acts and the Federal Elections Laws.

During the Hayes administration the latter laws were the subject of a prolonged and violent contest between the Democratic houses and the Republican President. The Democrats put great stress on the terror and intimidation of the whites and the violation of freemen's rights due to the presence of federal officials at the polls, and of federal troops near them. The Republicans insisted that these officials and troops were essential to enable the negroes to vote and to have their votes counted. As a matter of fact, neither of these contentions was of the highest significance so far as the South was concerned. The whites, once in control of the state electoral machinery, readily devised means of evading or neutralizing the influence of the federal officers. But the patronage in the hands of the administration party under these laws was enormous. The power to appoint supervisors and deputy marshals at election time was a tower of strength, from the point of view of direct votes and of indirect influence. Accordingly, the attack of the Democrats upon the laws was actuated mainly by the purpose of breaking down the Republican party organization in the South. The attack was successful in Mr. Hayes's time only to the extent that no appropriation was made for the payment of the supervisors and deputy marshals for their services in the elections of 1880. The system of federal supervision remained, but gradually lost all significance save as a biennial sign that the Republican party still survived, and when Mr. Cleveland became President even this relation to its original character disappeared.

The Force Acts experienced a similar decline during the period we are considering. In 1875, just before the Republicans lost control of Congress, they passed, as a sort of memorial to Charles Sumner, who had long urged its adoption, a Supplementary Civil Rights Bill, which made criminal, and put under the jurisdiction of the federal courts, any denial of equality to negroes in respect to accommodations in theatres, railway cars, hotels, and other such places. This was not regarded by the most thoughtful Republicans as a very judicious piece of legislation; but it was perceived that, with the Democrats about to control the House of Representatives, there was not likely to be a further opportunity for action in aid of the blacks, and so the act was permitted to go through and take its chances of good. Already, however, the courts had manifested a disposition to question the constitutionality of the most drastic provisions of the earlier Enforcement Acts. It has been said above that indictments under these acts had been many, but convictions few. Punishments were fewer still; for skillful counsel were ready to test the profound legal questions involved in the legislation, and numbers of cases crept slowly up on appeal to the Supreme Court. In 1875, this tribunal threw out an indictment under which a band of whites who had broken up a negro meeting in Louisiana had been convicted of conspiring to prevent negroes from assembling for lawful purposes and from carrying arms; for the right to assemble and the right to bear arms, the court declared, pertained to citizenship of a state, not of the United States, and therefore redress for interference with these rights must be sought in the courts of the state. In the same year, in the case of United States *v.* Reese, two sections of the Enforcement Act of 1870 were declared unconstitutional, as involving the exercise by the United States of powers in excess of those granted by the Fifteenth Amendment. It was not, however, till 1882 that the bottom was taken wholly out of the Ku Klux Act. In the case of United States *v.* Harris the conspiracy clause in its entirety was declared unconstitutional. This was a case from Tennessee, in which a band of whites had taken a negro away from the officers of the law and maltreated him. The court held that, under the last three amendments to the Constitution, Congress was authorized to guarantee equality in civil rights against violation by a state through its officers or agents, but not against violation by private individuals. Where assault or murder or other crime was committed by a private individual, even if the purpose was to deprive citizens of rights on the ground of race, the jurisdiction, and the exclusive jurisdiction, was in the state courts. And because the conspiracy clause brought such offenses into the jurisdiction of the United States it was unconstitutional and void. This decision finally disposed of the theory that the failure of a state to protect the negroes in their equal rights could be regarded as a positive denial of such rights, and hence could justify the United States in interfering. It left the blacks practically at the mercy of white public sentiment in the South. A year later, in 1883, the court summarily disposed of the act of 1875 by declaring that the rights which it endeavored to guarantee were not strictly civil rights at all, but rather social rights, and that in either case the federal government had nothing to do with them. The act was therefore held unconstitutional.

Thus passed the most characteristic features of the great system through which the Republicans had sought to prevent, by normal action of the courts, independently of changes in public opinion and political majorities, the undoing of reconstruction. Side by side with the removal of the preventives, the Southern whites had made enormous positive advances in the suppression of the other race. In a very general way, the process in this period, as contrasted with the earlier, may be said to have rested, in last resort, on legislation and fraud rather than on intimidation and force. The statute books of the states, especially of those in which negro rule had lasted the longest, abounded in provisions for partisan—that is, race—advantage. These were at once devoted as remorselessly to the extinction of black preponderance as they had been before to the repression of the whites. Moreover, by revision of the constitutions and by sweeping modifications of the laws, many strongholds of the old régime were destroyed. Yet, with all that could be done in this way, the fact remained that in many localities the negroes so greatly outnumbered the whites as to render the political ascendency of the latter impossible, except through some radical changes in the laws touching the suffrage and the elections; and in respect to these two points the sensitiveness of Northern feeling rendered open and decided action highly inexpedient. Before 1880 the anticipation, and after that year the realization, of a "solid South" played a prominent part in national politics. The permanence of white dominion in the South seemed, in view of the past, to depend as much on the exclusion of the Republicans from power at Washington as on the maintenance of white power at the state capitals. Under all the circumstances, therefore, extralegal devices had still to be used in the "black belt."

The state legislation which contributed to confirm white control included many ingenious and exaggerated applications of the gerrymander and the prescription of various electoral regulations that were designedly too intricate for the average negro intelligence. In Mississippi appeared the "shoestring district," three hundred miles long and about twenty wide, including within its boundaries nearly all the densest black communities of the state. In South Carolina, the requirement that, with eight or more ballot boxes before him, the voter must select the proper one for each ballot, in order to insure its being counted, furnished an effective means of neutralizing the ignorant black vote; for though the negroes, unable to read the lettering on the boxes, might acquire, by proper coaching, the power to discriminate among them by their relative positions, a moment's work by the whites in transposing the boxes would render useless an hour's laborious instruction. For the efficient working of this method of suppression, it was indispensable, however, that the officers of election should be whites. This suggests at once the enormous advantage gained by securing control of the state government. In the hot days of negro supremacy the electoral machinery had been ruthlessly used for partisan purposes, and when conditions were reversed the practice was by no means abandoned. It was, indeed, through their exclusive and carefully maintained control of the voting and the count that the whites found the best opportunities for illegal methods.

Because of these opportunities the resort to bulldozing and other violence steadily decreased. It penetrated gradually to the consciousness of the most brutal white politicians that the whipping or murder of a negro, no matter for what cause, was likely to become at once the occasion of a great outcry at the North, while by an unobtrusive manipulation of the balloting or the count very encouraging results could be obtained with little or no commotion. Hence that long series of practices, in regions where the blacks were numerous, that give so grotesque a character to the testimony in the contested-election cases in Congress, and to the reminiscences of candid Southerners. Polling places were established at points so remote from the densest black communities that a journey of from twenty to forty miles was necessary in order to vote; and where the roads were interrupted by ferries, the resolute negroes who attempted to make the journey were very likely to find the boats laid up for repairs. The number of polling places was kept so small as to make rapid voting indispensable to a full vote; and then the whites, by challenges and carefully premeditated quarrels among themselves, would amuse the blacks and consume time, till only enough remained for their own votes to be cast. The situation of the polls was changed without notice to the negroes, or, conversely, the report of a change was industriously circulated when none had been made. Open bribery on a large scale was too common to excite comment. One rather ingenious scheme is recorded which presents a variation on the old theme. In several of the states a poll-tax receipt was required as a qualification for voting. In an important local election, one faction had assured itself of the negro vote by a generous outlay in the payment of the tax for a large number of the blacks. The other faction, alarmed at the prospect of almost certain defeat, availed itself of the opportunity presented by the providential advent of a circus in the neighborhood, and the posters announced that poll-tax receipts would be accepted for admission. As a result, the audience at the circus was notable in respect to numbers, but the negro vote at the election was insignificant.

But exploitation of the poverty, ignorance, credulity, and general childishness of the blacks was supplemented, on occasion, by deliberate and high-handed fraud. Stuffing of the boxes with illegal ballots, and manipulation of the figures in making the count, were developed into serious arts. At the acme of the development undoubtedly stood the tissue ballot. There was in those days no prescription of uniformity in size and general character of the ballots. Hence miniature ballots of tissue paper were secretly prepared and distributed to trusted voters, who, folding as many, sometimes, as fifteen of the small tickets within one of the ordinary large tickets, passed the whole, without detection, into the box. Not till the box was opened were the tissue tickets discovered. Then, because the number of ballots exceeded the number of voters as indicated by the polling list, it became necessary, under the law, for the excess to be drawn out by a blindfolded man before the count began. So some one's eyes were solemnly bandaged, and he was set to drawing out ballots, on the theory that he could not distinguish those of one party from those of the other. The result is not hard to guess. In one case given by the Senate investigating committee, through whose action on the elections of 1878, in South Carolina, the theory and practice of the tissue ballot were revealed to an astonished world, the figures were as follows:

Number of ballots in box	1163
Names on polling list	620
Excess drawn out	543
Tissue ballots left to be counted	464

Not the least interesting feature of this episode was the explanation given by the white committee, of the existence of the great mass of tissue ballots. They were prepared, it was said, in order to enable the blacks who wished to vote the Democratic ticket to do so secretly, and thus to escape the ostracism and other social penalties which would be meted out to them by the majority of their race.

Under the pressure applied by all these various methods upon the negroes, the black vote slowly disappeared. And with it the Republican party faded into insignificance. In the presidential election of 1884 the total vote in South Carolina was, in round numbers, 91,000, as compared with 182,000 in 1876. In Mississippi the corresponding decrease was from 164,000 to 120,000; in Louisiana, from 160,000 to 108,000. The Republican party organization was maintained almost exclusively through the holders of federal offices in the postal and revenue service. When, in 1885, a Democratic administration assumed power, this basis for continued existence was very seriously weakened, and the decline of the party was much accelerated. Save for a few judicial positions held over from early appointments, the national offices, like those of the states, were hopelessly removed from the reach of any Republican's ambition. A comparison of the congressional delegation from the states of the defunct Confederacy in the Forty-First Congress (1869–71) with that in the Fifty-First (1889–91) is eloquent of the transformation that the two decades had wrought: in the former, twenty out of the twenty-two Senators were Republican, and forty-four out of fifty-eight Representatives; in the latter, there were no Republican Senators, and but three Representatives.

Summarily, then, it may be said that the second period in the undoing of reconstruction ends with the political equality of the negroes still recognized in law, though not in fact, and with the Republican party, for all practical purposes, extinct in the South.

The third period has had for its task the termination of equal rights in law as well as in fact.

The decline of negro suffrage and of the Republican party in the South was the topic of much discussion in national politics and figured in the party platforms throughout the period from 1876 to 1888; but owing to the deadlock in the party control of the national legislature the discussion remained academic in character, and the issue was supplanted in public interest by the questions of tariff, currency, and monopoly. By the elections of 1888, however, the Republicans secured not only the presidency, but also a majority in each house of Congress. The deadlock of thirteen years was broken, and at once an effort was made to resume the policy of the Enforcement Acts. A bill was brought in that was designed to make real the federal control of elections. The old acts for this purpose were, indeed, still on the statute book, but their operation was farcical; the new project, while maintaining the general lines of the old, would have imposed serious restraints on the influences that repressed the negro vote, and would have infused some vitality into the moribund Republican party in the South. It was quickly demonstrated, however, that the time for this procedure had gone by. The bill received perfunctory support in the House of Representatives, where it passed by the regular party majority, but in the Senate it was rather contemptuously set aside by Republican votes. Public sentiment in the North, outside of Congress, manifested considerable hostility to the project, and its adoption as a party measure probably played a role in the tremendous reaction which swept the Republicans out of power in the House in 1890, and gave to the Democrats in 1892 the control of both houses of Congress and the presidency as well. The response of the Democrats to the futile project of their adversaries was prompt and decisive. In February, 1894, an act became law which repealed all existing statutes that provided for federal supervision of elections. Thus the last vestige disappeared of the system through which the political equality of the blacks had received direct support from the national government.

In the meantime, a process had been instituted in the Southern states that has given the most distinctive character to the last period in the undoing of reconstruction. The generation-long discussions of the political conditions in the South have evoked a variety of explanations by the whites of the disappearance of the black vote. These different explanations have of course all been current at all times since reconstruction was completed, and have embodied different degrees of plausibility and truth in different places. But it may fairly be said that in each of the three periods into which the undoing of reconstruction falls one particular view has been dominant and characteristic. In the first period, that of the Ku Klux and the Mississippi plan, it was generally maintained by the whites that the black vote was not suppressed, and that there was no political motive behind the disturbances that occurred. The victims of murder, bulldozing, and other violence were represented as of bad character and socially dangerous, and their treatment as merely incident to their own illegal and violent acts, and expressive of the tendency to self-help instead of judicial procedure, which had always been manifest in Southern life, and had been aggravated by the demoralization of war time. After 1877, when the falling off in the Republican vote became so conspicuous, the phenomenon was explained by the assertion that the negroes had seen the light, and had become Democrats. Mr. Lamar gravely maintained, in a famous controversy with Mr. Blaine, that the original Republican theory as to the educative influence of the ballot had been proved correct by the fact that the enfranchised race had come to recognize that their true interests lay with the Democratic party; the Republicans were estopped, he contended, by their own doctrine from finding fault with the result. A corollary of this idea that the negroes were Democrats was generally adopted later in the period, to the effect that, since there was practically no opposition to the democracy, the negroes had lost interest in politics. They had got on the road to economic prosperity, and were too busy with their farms and their growing bank accounts to care for other things.

Whatever of soundness there may have been in any of these explanations, all have been superseded, during the last decade, by another, which, starting with the candid avowal that the whites are determined to rule, concedes that the elimination of the blacks from politics has been effected by intimidation, fraud, and any other means, legal or illegal, that would promote the desired end. This admission has been accompanied by expressions of sincere regret that illegal means were necessary, and by a general movement toward clothing with the forms of law the disfranchisement which has been made a fact without them. In 1890, just when the Republicans in Congress were pushing their project for renewing the federal control of elections, Mississippi made the first step in the new direction. Her constitution was so revised as to provide that, to be a qualified elector, a citizen must produce evidence of having paid his taxes (including a poll tax) for the past two years, and must, in addition, "be able to read any section in the constitution of this state, or . . . be able to understand the same when read to him, or give a reasonable interpretation thereof." Much might be said in favor of such an alternative intelligence qualification in the abstract: the mere ability to read is far from conclusive of intellectual capacity. But the peculiar form of this particular provision was confessedly adopted, not from any consideration of its abstract excellence, but in order to vest in the election officers the power to disfranchise illiterate blacks without disfranchising illiterate whites. In practice, the white must be stupid indeed who cannot satisfy the official demand for a "reasonable interpretation," while the negro who can satisfy it must be a miracle of brilliancy.

Mississippi's bold and undisguised attack on negro suffrage excited much attention. In the South it met with practically unanimous approval among thoughtful and conscientious men, who had been distressed by the false position in which they had long been placed. And at the North, public opinion, accepting with a certain satirical complacency the confession of the Southerners that their earlier explanations of conditions had been false, acknowledged in turn that its views as to the political capacity of the blacks had been irrational, and manifested no disposition for a new crusade in favor of negro equality. The action of Mississippi raised certain questions of constitutional law which had to be tested before her solution of the race problem could be regarded as final. Like all the other seceded states, save Tennessee, she had been readmitted to representation in Congress, after reconstruction, on the express condition that her constitution should never be so amended as to disfranchise any who were entitled to vote under the existing provisions. The new amendment was a mere explicit violation of this condition. Further, so far as the new clause could be shown to be directed against the negroes as a race, it was in contravention of the Fifteenth Amendment. These legal points had been elaborately discussed in the state convention, and the opinion had been adopted that, since neither race, color, nor previous condition of servitude was made the basis of discrimination in the suffrage, the Fifteenth Amendment had no application, and that the prohibition to modify the constitution was entirely beyond the powers of Congress, and was therefore void. When the Supreme Court of the United States was required to consider the new clause of Mississippi's constitution, it adopted the views of the convention on these points, and sustained the validity of the enactment. There was still one contingency that the whites had to face in carrying out the new policy. By the Fourteenth Amendment it is provided that if a state restricts the franchise her representation in Congress shall be proportionately reduced. There was a strong sentiment in Mississippi, as there is throughout the South, that a reduction of representation would not be an intolerable price to pay for the legitimate extinction of negro suffrage. But loss of Congressmen was by no means longed for, and the possibility of such a thing was very carefully considered. The phrasing of the franchise clause may not have been actually determined with reference to this matter; but it is obvious that the application of the Fourteenth Amendment is, to say the least, not facilitated by the form used.

The action of Mississippi in 1890 throws a rather interesting light on the value of political prophecy, even when ventured upon by the most experienced and able politicians. Eleven years earlier, Mr. Blaine, writing of the possibility of disfranchisement by educational and property tests, declared: "But no Southern state will do this, and for two reasons: first, they will in no event consent to a reduction of representative strength; and, second, they could not make any disfranchisement of the negro that would not at the same time disfranchise an immense number of whites." How sadly Mr. Blaine misconceived the spirit and underrated the ingenuity of the Southerners Mississippi made clear to everybody. Five years later South Carolina dealt no less unkindly with Mr. Lamar, who at the same time with Mr. Blaine had dipped a little into prophecy on the other side. "Whenever," he said—"and the time is not far distant—political issues arise which divide the white men of the South, the negro, will divide, too. . . . The white race, divided politically, will want him to divide." Incidentally to the conditions which produced the Populist party, the whites of South Carolina, in the years succeeding 1890, became divided into two intensely hostile factions. The weaker manifested a purpose to draw on the negroes for support, and began to expose some of the devices by which the blacks had been prevented from voting. The situation had arisen which Mr. Lamar had foreseen, but the result was as far as possible from fullfilling his prediction. Instead of competing with its rival for the black vote, the stronger faction, headed by

Mr. Tillman, promptly took the ground that South Carolina must have a "white man's government," and put into effect the new Mississippi plan. A constitutional amendment was adopted in 1895 which applied the "understanding clause" for two years, and after that required of every elector either the ability to read and write or the ownership of property to the amount of three hundred dollars. In the convention which framed this amendment, the sentiment of the whites revealed very clearly, not only through its content, but especially through the frank and emphatic form in which it was expressed, that the aspirations of the negro to equality in political rights would never again receive the faintest recognition.

Since the action of South Carolina, two other states, Louisiana and North Carolina, have excluded the blacks from the suffrage by analogous constitutional amendments; and in two others still, Alabama and Virginia, conventions are considering the subject as this article goes to press (August, 1901). By Louisiana, however, a new method was devised for exempting the whites from the effect of the property and intelligence tests. The hereditary principle was introduced into the franchise by the provision that the right to vote should belong, regardless of education or property, to every one whose father or grandfather possessed the right on January 1, 1867. This "grandfather clause" has been adopted by North Carolina, also, and, in a modified form and for a very limited time, by the convention in Alabama. The basis for the hereditary right in this latter state has been found, not in the possession of the franchise by the ancestor, but in the fact of his having been a soldier in any war save that with Spain. As compared with the Mississippi device for evading the Fifteenth Amendment, the "grandfather clause" has the merit of incorporating the discrimination in favor of the whites in the written law rather than referring it to the discretion of the election officers. Whether the Supreme Court of the United States will regard it as equally successful in screening its real purpose from judicial cognizance remains to be seen.

With the enactment of these contsitutional amendments by the various states, the political equality of the negro is becoming as extinct in law as it has long been in fact, and the undoing of reconstruction is nearing completion. The many morals that may be drawn from the three decades of the process it is not my purpose to suggest. A single reflection seems pertinent, however, in view of the problems which are uppermost in American politics at present. During the two generations of debate and bloodshed over slavery in the United States, certain of our statesmen consistently held that the mere chattel relationship of man to man was not the whole of the question at issue. Jefferson, Clay, and Lincoln all saw more serious facts in the background. But in the frenzy of the war time public opinion fell into the train of the emotionalists, and accepted the teachings of Garrison and Sumner and Phillips and Chase, that abolition and negro suffrage would remove the last drag on our national progress. Slavery was abolished, and reconstruction gave the freedmen the franchise.

But with all the guarantees that the source of every evil was removed, it became obvious enough that the results were not what had been expected. Gradually there emerged again the idea of Jefferson and Clay and Lincoln, which had been hooted and hissed into obscurity during the prevalence of the abolitionist fever. This was that the ultimate root of the trouble in the South had been, not the institution of slavery, but the coexistence in one society of two races so distinct in characteristics as to render coalescence impossible; that slavery had been a *modus vivendi* through which social life was possible; and that, after its disappearance, its place must be taken by some set of conditions which, if more humane and beneficent in accidents, must in essence express the same fact of racial inequality. The progress in the acceptance of this idea in the North has measured the progress in the South of the undoing of reconstruction. In view of the questions which have been raised by our lately established relations with other races, it seems most improbable that the historian will soon, or ever, have to record a reversal of the conditions which this process has established.

Concluding
Commentary

BLISS PERRY

With the paper on The Undoing of Reconstruction, in the present issue of the Atlantic, its series of articles upon the reconstruction period comes to a close. The theme of these papers seems to us so important, and their bearing upon our immediate political future so significant, that we venture to remind our readers of some of the truths suggested by these studies of a troubled epoch.

The frankness of the authors of the reconstruction articles has been noticeable. Representing many sections of the country and many varieties of political opinion, they were asked to review the conditions upon which the Southern states were readmitted to the Union after the close of the Civil War. Some of the writers, like ex-Secretary Herbert and ex-Governor Chamberlain, fought in the war, and played a personal part in the events that followed it. Mr. McCall, the biographer of Thaddeus Stevens, had had occasion to make a careful study of the congressional side of the reconstruction controversy. Mr. Thomas Nelson Page had already illustrated, in his chosen art of fiction, the temper of the Southern people during reconstruction times. Mr. William Garrott Brown and Mr. Phelps had utilized unusual opportunities for studying particular phases of the period in different sections of the South. Professor Du Bois, who wrote upon The Freedmen's Bureau, had won a reputation among economists for his careful statistical studies of his race. Professor Woodrow Wilson, who began the series, and Professor Dunning, who now closes it, are historians known for their luminous presentation of the vexed questions involved in the reconstruction policy. All of these writers had, of course, the fullest liberty to express their personal opinions. More than thirty years have passed since the legislation of 1870 completed the formal processes of reconstruction, and in spite of the passionate political feelings involved in every step of that procedure, the Atlantic articles have been written both dispassionately and, we believe, with entire candor. Many political motives, hitherto more or less veiled, have been laid bare, but there has been no attempt by the authors of these papers to palliate the errors committed by both North and South, in that confused and trying hour of our national history. They have recognized that we are living in a new age, and that Americans, united by a new national spirit, can now discuss with calmness the mistakes made a generation ago.

The most grave of these errors was the indiscriminate bestowal of the franchise upon the newly liberated slaves. The extent to which partisan purposes entered into the adoption of this policy will always be disputed. Mr. McCall has presented the accepted views of Northern Republicans in upholding the measure as a political necessity. Necessary to the immediate security of a great and victorious party it may have been; certainly, it was in part a sincere, idealistic effort to render abstract justice to a race that had been deeply wronged. But it is apparent enough today that the sudden gift of the ballot to men wholly unprepared to use it wisely was a most dangerous policy, however well intentioned it may have been. It is equally apparent that, in so far as partisan motive was dominant in the transaction, partisanship has paid the penalty. The "solid South" is still solid. Reconstruction, particularly in its earlier phases, brought such widespread demoralization to the Southern states that its economic losses are comparable to those of the Civil War. In fact, the whole scheme of reconstruction, so skillfully and in part nobly planned, so boldly carried out, has broken down. Professor Dunning traces for us the various stages that have characterized the systematic undoing of that which was supposed to have been done once for all. He shows precisely how it has come about that in the South to-day "the negroes enjoy practically no political rights; the Republican party is but the shadow of a name; and the influence of the negroes in political affairs is nil." The constitutional conventions in session during the past summer, in various Southern states, have had for their chief and openly avowed purpose the elimination of the negro from politics, or, in Professor Dunning's phrase, making the political equality of the negro "as extinct in law as it has long been in fact." The final stage of the long reconstruction controversy seems to close, singularly enough, in the reversal of the very process which marked its inception. Reconstruction began with enfranchisement; it is ending with disfranchisement.

Who are left to mourn over this withdrawal of political rights from the negro? There are at least four classes who regret it: (1) Intelligent leaders of that race, who recognize that in the breakdown of negro popular suffrage the industrious, property-holding, educated black is likely to suffer the same disability as the ignorant and vicious. This is the intention and the practical result of much of the disfranchising legislation already consummated, however adroitly the fact may be concealed. (2) Active friends of the negro at the North, spiritual descendants of the abolitionists—men and women who have never wearied, and surely will never weary, in their efforts to uplift the blacks.

These people are giving largely for negro education, of both the industrial and academic type. Though comparatively few in numbers, they command considerable influence, and they resent the forced closure of any avenue that opens the way for negro self-respect and training in self-government. (3) Some Republicans of the old sort, like those of Iowa lately assembled in convention, who are still faithful to the doctrine of equal rights, and opposed to "all legislation designed to accomplish the disfranchisement of citizens upon lines of race, color, or station in life." (4) And a good many persons, North and South, of all parties and no party, who believe that the experiment of republican government in this country is secure only in so far as its fundamental principle of self-government by the masses is allowed unimpeded scope.

Who rejoice over the enforced retirement of the negro from politics? There are assuredly four classes here: (1) A horde of ignorant "poor whites," mostly of pure "Anglo-Saxon" stock, who are being outstripped in the march of civilization even by the negroes, and who imagine that a "grandfather clause" will save them from the consequences of illiteracy and degeneracy. They are the most pitiable and the most dangerous element in our composite national life. (2) Southern Democratic politicians. (3) The majority of the Southern people, of whom it should be said that they understand the Southern negro as no Northerners can, and who are at least as kindly disposed toward him as the masses of the Northern people. (4) A good many persons, again of all parties and no party, who secretly rejoice at any expression of the racial superiority of the Anglo-Saxon; who believe, not in a democratic government, in which all citizens shall participate upon precisely the same terms, but in a "strong" or "white man's" government. These people are Americans by accident of birth, but politically they are Europeans, aristocrats and reactionists.

Between these friends and foes of disfranchisement stands a

vast body of indifferentists. Some of the indifference is found, it is true, among well-wishers of the colored people, who think that as long as their economical and industrial rights are assured the blacks had better "keep out of politics;" forgetting how closely, in an industrial democracy like our own, political and industrial rights are bound together. The masses of the North belong also to the indifferent class. Northern political feeling upon the negro question, to be effective, must be fused by one of those furnace-glows of moral passion such as was felt forty years ago. Our temporary coldness to the moral issues involved in politics, combined with that world-wide reaction against democracy which has been noted by many recent Atlantic writers, makes it unlikely that any considerable portion of the Northern public will at present seriously bestir themselves in the negro's behalf.

Nor can he look for help to either of the two great national parties. The leaders of the party of emancipation and reconstruction have apparently decided that it is inexpedient to interfere with what is taking place in the South. Occasional state conventions, like that of Iowa, already referred to, will doubtless reaffirm the historic Republican position with regard to equal rights, and the next national platform will probably contain an unexceptionable and smoothly planed plank of the same texture. There the matter will end. The Democratic party, demoralized at best and absolutely dependent upon the Southern vote, can offer no hope to the negro. The spectacle of Southern Democrats passing resolutions asserting the right of Filipinos to self-government, and at the same instant refusing self-government to men of dark-skinned race in America, was one of the broad jokes of the last campaign. Indeed, it must be confessed that our present national insistence upon our right to administer the affairs of other races, in our newly acquired territory, makes it extremely embarrassing for either party to urge a literal obedience to the Fifteenth Amendment in the South. Whatever blessings our acquisition of foreign territory may bring in the future, its influence upon equal rights in the United States has already proved malign. It has strengthened the hands of the enemies of negro progress, and has postponed further than ever the realization of perfect equality of political privilege. If the stronger and cleverer race is free to impose its will upon "new-caught, sullen peoples" on the other side of the globe, why not in South Carolina and Mississippi? The advocates of the "shot-gun policy" are quite as sincere, and we are inclined to think quite as unselfish, as the advocates of "benevolent assimilation." The two phrases are, in fact, two names for the same thing: government by force—the absolute determination by one race of the extent of political privilege to be enjoyed by another. There is a great deal to be said for this theory of government, in cases where a civilized people have assumed control of an un-civilized people, and at present it has more friends than at any other time since the close of the Napoleonic wars. But it is not a theory which bodes good to the full manhood of the American negro.

What, then, must be the immediate programme and the ulti-mate hope of those who believe, as the Atlantic does, in the old-fashioned American doctrine of political equality, irrespective of race or color or station? The short cut to equality, attempted by giving the negro the ballot before he was qualified to use it, has proved disastrous. It has confused the issue, and cast doubt upon the principle of equality itself. The long way around must now be tried—the painfully slow but certain path that leads through labor and education and mutual understanding and un-imagined patience to the goal of full political privilege. . . . [W]e may be allowed to point out here what we believe to be the surest ground for hope in the final victory of equal rights.

That hope lies in the good sense of the South. It is obvious that she is being left to herself, to settle the question of disfran-chisement in her own way. Terribly destructive of the public respect for law as is her unhindered violation of the letter and spirit of the Constitution, disheartening as it is to see some blatant and brutal Tillman take up again the old cry of "Down with the niggers!" all this may be preferable, in the long view, to another epoch of forcible intervention. The South must learn by her own blunders, as she has had to do ere now. Thrown upon her own responsibility, and freed from the jealous fear of Northern interference, there is ground for confidence that she will yet follow her innate sense of justice and of honor. Under normal conditions, she possesses these characteristics to as high a degree as any portion of the Union. Grossly unfair and cruel as the conduct of Southern politicians toward the negro has often been, it is no worse treatment than Northern politicians would have given him, under similar temptation. Remorselessly as the "color line" is drawn in the Southern states, it is scarcely less rigid in the North, save in this one matter of the ballot.

At all events, the South is justified in the inference that the country is now willing, for one reason or another, to give her a chance to show her real temper. Southern whites are already making manly confession of the evil that has been wrought upon themselves, no less than upon the blacks, by the systematic falsification of election returns. They are doubtless right in believing that open, avowed suppression of the negro vote—if that vote is to be eliminated—is better for all concerned than a scheme of fraud and chicanery. But some degree of chicanery there must be in each of these new legal devices for contravening the express purpose of the Fifteenth Amendment, and we believe that Southerners will one day take a still more manly and American position, and admit to all the privileges of citizenship any man who proves himself worthy of it. This will require sacrifice of sentiment and tradition. Many years are likely to pass, and possibly many generations, before such a result is attained. But we believe there is too much potential intelligence in the South, and too much love of fair play, permanently to refuse the ballot to colored men of education and property who have attested their value to the community.

Apply to both races equally whatever qualifications for the exercise of the franchise or for holding office each state may see fit to impose: that is the only demand which can wisely be made upon the South. We think she will ultimately grant it, not only because it is the bidding of good sense and of good faith, but also because any other course will mean her moral suicide. To fall back upon a "grandfather clause"—to refuse the ballot to a colored farmer or artisan of intelligence and property, and grant it to some illiterate pauper because he is white—is to put a premium upon the ignorance of one race, and a discount upon the progress of the other. The Southern negroes, in spite of every shortcoming and disadvantage, are slowly, but surely, making headway. Every consideration, whether of economics or of humanity, demands that they should have an open road. They will do the traveling.

Mr. Thomas Nelson Page closed his survey of reconstruction, in the preceding number of this magazine, with these admirable words: "That intelligence, virtue, and force of character will eventually rule is as certain in the states of the South as it is elsewhere; and everywhere it is as certain as the operation of the law of gravitation. Whatever people wish to rule in those states must possess these qualities." His tacit assumption, no doubt, is that it will be the whites who are to exhibit these dominant qualities. Yet we imagine that Booker Washington would wish no better motto for the encouragement of his people than those words of Mr. Page. For "intelligence, virtue, and force of character" are not the endowment of the Anglo-Saxon exclusively. Their roots sink deeper than those of racial peculiarity into the soil of our common humanity. The race that does not bring them to flower is indeed doomed; and whatever race develops intelligence, virtue, and force by ceaseless moral effort will in due season reap the reward. But in such a noble strife as this each race may help the other. It has hitherto been the curse of the South that she has contained two races living in abnormal relations toward each other. Yet it is not impossible that, remaining, in the terms of Booker Washington's famous sentence, "in all things purely social as separate as the fingers, yet one as the hand in all things essential to mutual progress," these races may ultimately give not only a signal example of mutual service, but unexpected reinforcement to the old faith that the plain people, of whatever blood or creed, are capable of governing themselves.

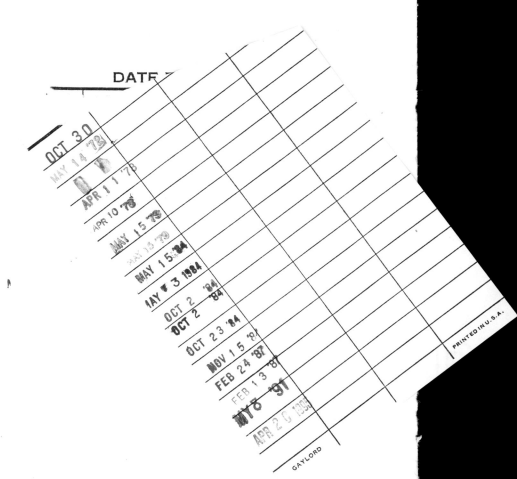